SUPER KITES III

by

NEIL THORBURN

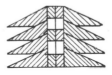

PHOTOGRAPHS

By author and Donald Ray except as noted in text.

Parts of this book are excerpts or
revisions of sections of Super Kites,
a 20 page pamphlet, 1975; and Super
Kites II, a 112 page book, 1983.

Library of Congress Catalog Number 84-164133

ISBN 0-9629354-3-3

ACKNOWLEDGEMENTS

Thanks to the following for aiding and abetting the making of this book:

Family—

My wife, Adell, for long sufferance of my folly, my son, Gene, for years of flying companionship and the use of the shop, my daughter, Lynne, for the use of her back yard flight pad, my daughter, Sandra, for her perennial enthusiasm and spirited kite flying, my son-in-law, Waine Landers, for his zoom lense and superb photographs, my son-in-law, Virgle Ray, for his photography, kiteflying, and electronic expertese, my daughter-in-law, Victoria, for editorial assistance and typing, my grandson, Don, for building and flying kites so well, my grandson, Greg, for his kiteflying and his drawings, my grandson, Paul, for his old pro kite handling, my grandchildren, Douglas, Jennifer, and twins, David and Katie, for being such interested lineholders. Greatgrand-daughter, Mandy,* and Dawn, her kiteflying mother, can help on the next book. *Mandy won a prize at age 5 in San Francisco-adult event.

Kiteflying friends—

- H.B. Alexander for encouragement, kite design, photos, and poetry.
- Oscar Bailey, Bruce Kennington, and others who built and won prizes at major kiting events with their versions of Super Kite designs.
- Wayne Baldwin for his early on order and letter and his keeping the ancient art of Filipino kites alive.
- Jon Bloom for winning two kite contests in a row in England with his Pagoda and sending a picture of his beautiful kite.
- The girl from Idaho, whose letter I lost and whose name I can never remember and who looked me up at a Santa Clara kite fly,
- Valerie Govig, editor of Kite Lines, for the 8 by 10 glossy and for building a Stacked Deltas, winning with it at Nags Head, and writing of her triumph.
- Shakib Gunn, Singapore, for the most distant and last order.
- Gary Hinze for hours of kiting together, expert advice, and his kite.
- Those kiteflying dentists in Italy.
- Jerome Prager for the Filipino kite plan.
- Richard Robertson, Austin, TX, for great photos of his Super Kites.
- Leland Toy, editor of Kite Flyer, for publicity and not too gentle urging to get this book published.
- Bernice Turner for her poems.
- AKA officers for prompt and courteous assistance.
- Tom and Moira Caldwell and George and Marion Ham for their competition, camaraderie and beautiful kites.
- The Kite & Balloon Company, London, England, and their clientel- Super Kites' best customers.
- All others, from Kitimat, BC to Aukland, New Zealand who risked $2.50 on a 20 page pamphlet. Let us hope there is more for their money this time, and especially those who made necessary this reissue.

CONTENTS

WHY KITES?

Fascination with kites in the days before the mastery of the skies through powered flight is understandable. It was an opportunity for communication with the broad firmament of heaven, even as the fowls. But when shining ships pass every hour, high above the limits of any kite, and manned flight to the moon appear on television, why do mankind's first experiments in aerodonetics yet arouse our curiosity and excite our imagination?

It may be the many and varied activities that are a part of kiting. One may engage in kite fighting, engage in the athletics of guided kites in train, loft art forms, seek records in altitude or size, or, like most of us, hold to the end of a line and watch and feel our kite reacting to the air currents. Perhaps David Copperfield's description of fiction's best known kite flyer, the lovable, eccentric, and much troubled Mr. Dick, provides enough reason to fly a kite.

> It was quite an affecting sight, I used to think, to see him when it was up a great height in the air. What he had told me in his room, about it disseminating the the statements pasted on it, which were nothing but old leaves of abortive Memorials, might have been a fancy with him sometimes, but not when he was out, looking up at the kite in the sky, and feeling it pull and tug at his hand. He never look so serene as he did then. I used to fancy, as I sat with him 'of an evening, on a green slope, and saw him watch the kite high in the quiet air, that it lifted his mind out of its confusion and bore it......into the skies.

Did Dickens, at some time, send his perplexities and confusions up a kite string? Can we do the same?

There are two general catagories of kiters; those who just fly kites and those, like Mr. Dick, who prefer to loft their own creations. This book should have something for both groups but more for the latter, since the kite designs on the various pages are original and do not appear in other kite books nor can they be found in kite stores. The kites have been designed for striking appearance and outstanding performance.

Performance, to the kite sophisticate, usually includes the following:

1. The kite flies at a steep angle while maintaining a taut line.
2. The kite flies in a wide range of winds, from light to heavy, and shows good stability throughout.

In order to attain these characteristics, the kites have their stability built in (no tails needed), and are planned for maximum strength with minimum weight. A famous racing yacht designer once quipped that the only vehicle whose performance was improved by increasing weight was a steam roller. If the adage is true for boats, it doubly applies to kites.

The plans call for readily available and economical materials-plastic trash bags, pine or spruce sticks, bamboo plant support stakes, etc.-and require common tools and skills. True, these kites are not for the beginner, with a pair of scissors, a pot of paste, and an evening to wile away. They demand precise measurements, careful workmanship, and time. The kites are also adaptable to other covering materials such as cloth or Tyvek.

Several of the designs have proved their mettle on this continent and abroad. The Pagoda, which appeared in the twenty page pamphlet, *Super Kites* in 1975, has won top honors in several competitions. The Stacked Deltas, which was featured in the winter, 1976-77 issue of the magazine *Kite Lines*, won top prize at Nags Head, NC the following year. It was built and flown by Valerie Govig, the magazine's editor, her first big win. The other kites described in the book are new types that are as good or better than those mentioned and should give kite buffs many pleasurable hours of building and flying.

This book, then, is not another overview of kiting, repeating fact and fallacy from other sources and reiterated plans from other books but is, rather, a venture in in new directions for the adventurous kiter. Philosophy, history, theory, etc. are confined to the illustrations and poetry in the book

WINGED BOXES

Lawrence Hargrave's invention of the box kite in 1892 was the first modern breakaway from traditional kite design. He built a self-stabilized kite-no tail-that could fly in strong winds and reach great altitudes. His experiments were known and heeded by the Wrights and other aeronautical pioneers, and his kites were standard equipment for U.S. meteorologists for years. Hargrave and others varied the original design in many ways, and today's kiters are still modifying the box kite.

THE STUB WING BOX

This kite is an old example of augmenting an existing type to enhance performance and aspect. The corner flown box is a windy, stogy performer that can at best be desribed as stable, dependable, and rugged. Its faults include a tendency toward overweight and a proclivity to fly at a slant and to veer to one side. In order to make it straighten up and fly right, the transverse diagonal should be be made longer than the fore-and-aft diagonal. This presents a more obtuse angle to the wind, more

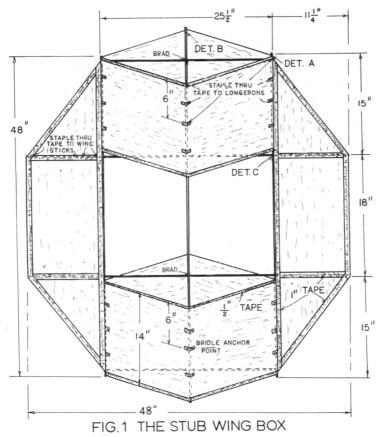

FIG.1 THE STUB WING BOX

9

surface for lift, and the kite flies straighter and better. Note: The covering is specified as plastic trash bags. Tyvek or other fabrics that can be taped, glued, or heat sealed will follow naturally. Those who prefer cloth should be able to adapt the designs to the sewing machine.

MATERIALS

2 4'X33" plastic trash bags
8 4'X$\frac{1}{4}$"X$\frac{1}{4}$" spruce or pine sticks
2 4'X $\frac{1}{4}$" strips of bamboo fencing
strong cord, thread, white glue, duct tape
plastic coffee can lid

CONSTRUCTION PROCEDURE

1. Tack a 4'X 33" trash bag to a level surface. Fully extend the bag with no wrinkles.
2. Trim and square top of bag and draw lines across bag at 14" and 28" with a permanent ink felt pen.
3. Draw location lines down center of bag as in FIG.2. Make sure the line is equidistant from both edges of the bag at all locations, since there is a slight variation in width in most bags. Transfer the location lines to the other side of the cells by impressions with a ball point pen. Draw lines on other side.

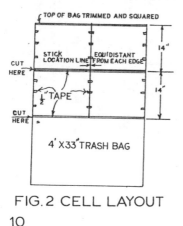

FIG.2 CELL LAYOUT

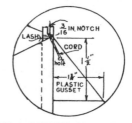

DET. A CORNER GUSSET

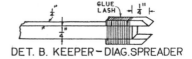

DET. B. KEEPER—DIAG. SPREADER

10

4. Apply tape to the cells with no wrinkles in the tape or plastic. It is easier to tape while the bag remains tacked. Apply to the tops and bottoms of the cells to within an inch of the edge of the bag. Cut cells out as in FIG. 2, remove tacks, turn cells over, retack, tape other side and draw location lines. Spread cells so the taping of the circumferences can be finished using short pieces of tape.

5. Staple cells to 4 ft. sticks, $\frac{1}{4}$ inch from the ends, FIG. 1. Stretch cells slightly while stapling. Use the creased edges of the bag as location lines for two sticks.

    Note: When a covering of cloth or Tyvek is used, the cells may be formed around a cardboard 33 in. wide.

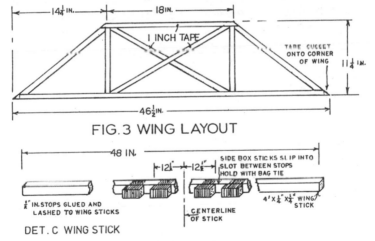

FIG. 3 WING LAYOUT

DET. C WING STICK

6. Lash and glue stops to two 48 in. wing sticks (DET. C) Fix a $\frac{1}{4}$ in. strip of bamboo to the backs of the wing sticks with glue and thread lashing the length of the stick.

7. Trim $2\frac{1}{4}"X\frac{1}{4}"$ sticks to 25 inches. Lash $1"X\frac{1}{4}"X\frac{1}{8}"$ retainers to the ends, DET. B.

8. Partially assemble the box with the 25"sticks 1"away from the top and bottom and the wing sticks 15" away. Retain the wing sticks at the stops with bag ties or string.

9. The fore-and-aft braces are now prepared. They are four in number and around 21" long and $\frac{1}{4}$"x $\frac{1}{4}$" stock. They may vary in length at the different locations due to irregularities of the bag. Trim each brace to fit at its location so the stick flexes slightly when the box is extended. Fix retainers to ends, DET. B. and extend the box.

10. Lay out and trim two wings on another tacked down bag and apply the tape, wrinkle free. Tape on gussets (DET. A.) and drill holes as shown. Thread a strong cord through the holes and tie so the loops seat in the notches with the wing under tension. Three fourths or a half inch stretch to the wing should do it.

11. Staple the wings to the wing sticks with a paper stapler, starting inboard, keeping the wing taut, and stapling every three inches.

12. Brad cross braces together at centers.

13. Tie 30 lb. test string to bridle points, FIG.1. The loop should be about 18 in. from the top point, 40 in. from the bottom point. These distances may be varied according to wind velocity; higher for a blow, lower in light winds.

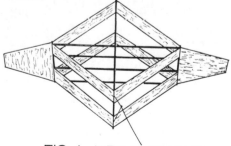

FIG.4 KITE IN FLIGHT

Another Way to Rig a Stub Wing Box

The theory motivating this variation was as follows:

If a corner flown box kite's performance is improved when the transverse diagonal is longer than the fore-and-aft diagonal, increasing the disproportion should further improve performance.

The disproportion was increased to a ratio of two to one, and the theory proved valid, and the kite flew like crazy. However, as is commonly the case in a design alterations, a new problem arose. The internal stresses, which are considerable in a "Stub", were increased by the alterations. This meant stronger cross bracing and wing spars, which increased weight. In order to keep the weight in line, bamboo cross bracing was devised from plant support stakes to take advantage of their high strength to weight ratio.

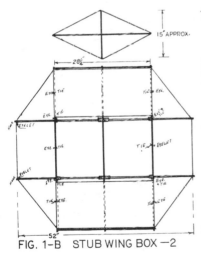

FIG. 1-B   STUB WING BOX —2

MATERIALS

1. Covering and longerons are the same dimensions as Stub Wing Box (page 9 , FIG 1   )
2. Six 3ft. bamboo stakes.
3. Eyelets, heavy paper clips, plastic lid, vent tape, etc..

CONSTRUCTION

1. If Tyvec is used, fold and glue half inch hem or glue inch re-enforcing strip at tape locations. Apply small patches of tape on each side of material at eyelets.
2. Select 4 stakes with approx. one fourth in. dia. at the large

13

end. They should be as straight as possible and have the same stiffness. To test for stiffness, place small end of stake on a bathroom scale and push straight down with your fingertip until the stake bends. Reading the scale will show the stiffness. 4 or 5 lbs. is sufficient.

3. Insert eyelets at locations on inner edge of wings and at the two outboard corners. Tie wings to longs.

4. Ream $\frac{1}{2}$" to $\frac{5}{8}$" dia. by 4" long bamboo for a snug fit for the large ends of the stakes. Lash stub with glue and thread and insert the stakes. Split two inch rounds of bamboo and glue and lash in place as below:

Hook   Hook

|←——————— 28¼" ———————→|

5. Tie the wing struts in place so the side longs are held apart by the stops and trim the struts so that hooks inserted in the ends will, when hooked through the outboard eyelets, extend the wings until taut.

6. Trim and prepare 2 fore-and-aft braces to extend the cells at the wing spars

7. Select 2 stakes of approx. $\frac{3}{16}$" dia. and with as little taper as can be found. Drill holes to accept brads in the side longs $\frac{3}{16}$" from the ends. Trim the stakes to $28\frac{1}{4}$" and slip the holes in the ends over the brads. Prepare and install fore-and-aft braces to extend the cells at the ends. The fore-and-aft braces can be of either pine sticks or bamboo stakes. If pine is used, lash retainers to the ends. Use brads with bamboo. A stop should be glued or lashed to the f.&a. braces so they may be tied at the center. Monofilament "springs" keep the f. & a. braces snug. (See p.39, No.7 & FIG. 29).

8. Bridle as Stub Wing Box, pg.12, No.13.

THE DELTA WING BOX

Hanging a delta wing on a corner flown box is a great combination of talents. The stability of the central box provides a solid platform for the graceful, efficient, delta wing. It produces a 30% gain in area with only 15% weight increase.

There are several construction procedures used for this kite that will be employed in building other kites in the book. The strip retainers that hold the wings to the longerons make many kites buildable. The bamboo support stake spreader is hard to top for strength when its light weight is considered.

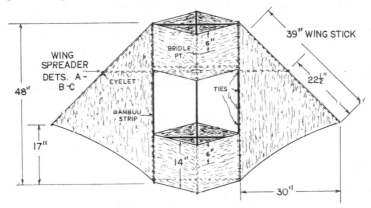

FIG. 5 THE DELTA WING BOX

MATERIALS

2 4' X 33" trash bags
10 4' X $\frac{1}{4}$" X $\frac{1}{4}$" spruce or pine sticks
2 3' bamboo stakes approx. $\frac{5}{16}$" to $\frac{3}{8}$" dia.. Also a 3" to 4" stub of bamboo approx. $\frac{1}{2}$" dia.
2 drape hooks or jumbo paper clips, white glue, thread, light twine, staples, duct tape
2 thin bamboo strips 4' long

CONSTRUCTION

1. Prepare the cells and longs. in the same way as that of the STUB WING BOX and assemble box.
2. Make four sets of cross braces approx. 25" across by 21" fore-and-aft.
3. Assemble the box section with cross braces.
4. Lay out wings on a 4' X 33" plastic bag, FIG. 6.

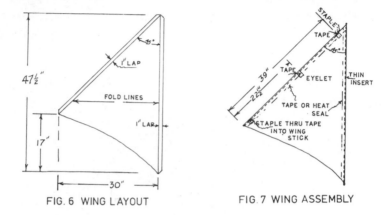

FIG. 6 WING LAYOUT   FIG. 7 WING ASSEMBLY

5. Transfer the location lines with a ball point pen. Cut out wings.
6. Draw loc. lines on other wing.
7. Tack the wing to a flat surface and tape or heat seal to form hem slots. Polyethylene plastic can be sealed with a burning iron, soldering iron, or a pressing iron if paper is kept between the hot iron and plastic, and the iron is pressed along the seam at the right speed. Practice on scrap plastic perfects this technique. I use the edge of an old pressing iron.
8. Apply tape patches as in FIG. 7.
9. Slip the wing spars into their sockets. Staple at the tape patches into the wing spars. Fix the spreader eyelets at locations. If you do not have an eyelet tool, punch a hole through several layers of tape instead. See FIG. 7.

10. Prepare two inserts for the inboard sockets of the wings. These can be of thin bamboo since they do not provide structural strength. Their only function is to hold the wings to the longs. To keep the strips in their slots, run tape from the wings, over the ends of the strips, and back to the wings so as to put a slight stretch to the plastic.

11. Tie the wings to the longs. with a needle and light twine. Sew through the plastic of both the box and the wing, around the strip and the long, and tie securely with a surgeon's square knot.

12. Select two stakes from a packet of 3 foot bamboo with approx. $\frac{5}{16}$" dia. at the large ends and of similar taper. Find another stake with a diameter approx. $\frac{1}{2}$ inch and cut off a three to four inch stub.(DET. D and E) Lash the stub with thread and glue and ream the hole in the stub with a drill to a diameter that accepts the large ends of the stakes with a press fit.

13. Assemble the spreader and insert drapery hooks or hook made from jumbo paper clips. (DET. E)

14. Trim the stakes so the wings are fully extended so

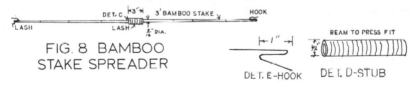

FIG. 8 BAMBOO
STAKE SPREADER

as to be taut but not so taut as to put a bend in the spreader.

15. Tie a bridle of 40 lb. test line to the points. The top leg should be about 16 inches to the loop and the bottom leg about 31 inches.

17

2

WINGED CONYNES

After Hargrave came Conyne. The triangular box provided an excellent stabilizer for a wing that offered an effective area the wind without the inhibiting drag of a tail. The relatively narrow width of the center made a lighter wing spar practical than on a winged box.

.The basic Conyne is covered in other books, so there are no plans for it here. However, a Conyne could be put together of plastic in the same way as is the Stub Wing Box with the taped and stapled wings and the gussets of "lid" plastic in the corners.

THE DELTA WING CONYNE

MATERIALS

1   4 ft. x 33 in. trash bag
4   $\frac{1}{8}"$ x 30$\frac{1}{2}"$ spruce or pine sticks and –
1   $\frac{3}{16}"$ x $\frac{1}{4}"$ stick, or –
3   $\frac{3}{16}"$ x 30$\frac{1}{2}"$ dowels and 2 $\frac{1}{8}"$ x 30$\frac{1}{2}"$ dowels.
2   $\frac{1}{4}"$ x $\frac{1}{4}"$ x 36" sticks or 2 $\frac{1}{4}$ x 36" dowels
2   24" by $\frac{1}{4}"$ dia. bamboo stakes – tape, twine, etc.

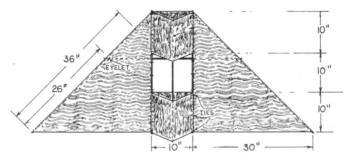

FIG. 9   THE DELTA WING CONYNE

CONSTRUCTION

1. Lay out wings and cells on the trash bag, FIG. 10.
2. Draw construction lines and transfer them by indentation to the underside of the bag.
3. Cut out the wings and cells a draw location lines on the under side of the wing and the bottom cell.
4. Tack wings and cells to a flat surface and heat seal or tape the stick slots as shown.
5. Apply tape to wings and cells, FIG. 11 & DET. A. Fix tape on the edges of the cells and around the hems so the slots are re-enforced.

6. Insert the $37\frac{1}{2}''$ wing sticks into their slots and staple them in place through the tape patches.

7. Insert the spreader eyelets as shown.

8. Insert $30\frac{1}{2}''$ sticks or into cell hems. Hold them in place with short pieces of tape so they protrude $\frac{1}{4}$ in. over the ends of each cell.

9. Tape $30\frac{1}{2}'' \times \frac{1}{8}''$ sticks or dowels onto the back of wing, FIG. 11.

10. Fold the flaps at the vent over the longerons and tape or heat seal.

11. Lay the cell section on top of the wing so the longerons are aligned with the retaining sticks taped upon the

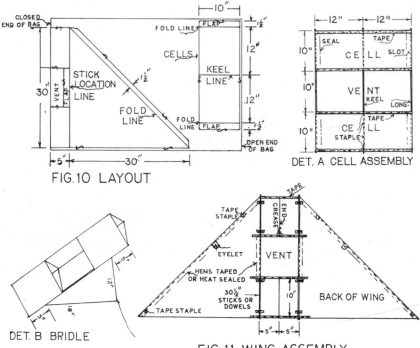

FIG. 10 LAYOUT

DET. A CELL ASSEMBLY

DET. B BRIDLE

FIG. 11 WING ASSEMBLY

20

back of the wing. Sandwich the sections together by tieing the longerons to the retainers every three or four inches. Use a needle and light twine so the ties go through the fabric, around the sticks, and knot at the back of the wing.

12. Staple the $\frac{3}{16}"$ x $\frac{1}{4}"$ x $30\frac{1}{2}"$ stick to the keel line with the staples entering the $\frac{3}{16}"$ edge, or tie a $\frac{3}{16}"$ dowell to the line by sewing through the tape and or fabric, around the dowell, and knotting firmly every 3 or 4 inches.

13. Prepare a bamboo wing spreader similar to the one used on the "Delta Wing Box", page 17, FIG.8. Select stakes of slightly smaller diameter since the spreader is shorter. A second sturdier spreader can be constructed and held in reserve for strong winds on any of the wide deltas, but there is no gain in overweighting the kite. The spreader is by necessity the weightiest spar on the kite.

14. Tie a bridle of 30 lb. test string to the keel, DET. B.

THE TWIN CONYNE DELTA

The construction of this kite is similar to the Delta Wing Conyne and it performs about the same when flown on a single line. However, the "Twin" is a natural for conversion to a guided kite with the addition of a short yoke at the bridle and a second string.

MATERIALS

The same materials are required as those in the Delta Wing Conyne with the following exceptions:
2 3'x$\frac{5}{16}"$ bamboo stakes for spreaders and a 3" by$\frac{1}{2}"$ bamboo stub for a center joiner.

A second set of longerons and wing retainers & another keel stick

4 3'x$\frac{1}{8}"$ dia. bamboo stakes for cross bracing the center section. $\frac{1}{8}"$ dowels or other light sticks can be substituted.

21

A second 4' x 33" plastic bag.
A 12" x $\frac{3}{16}$ x $\frac{3}{16}$" stick for a yoke.

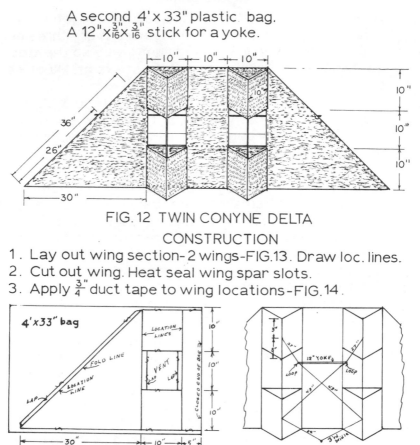

FIG. 12 TWIN CONYNE DELTA
CONSTRUCTION

1. Lay out wing section - 2 wings - FIG. 13. Draw loc. lines.
2. Cut out wing. Heat seal wing spar slots.
3. Apply $\frac{3}{4}$" duct tape to wing locations - FIG. 14.

FIG. 13 WING LAYOUT

DET. A BRIDLE

4. Tape retainers to back of wing section. Staple delta wing spars in place. FIG. 14
5. Cut out 4 cells (pg. 20, FIG. 10). Seal sockets and tape as in the Delta Wing Conyne.
6. Assemble 2 boxes - pg.   DET. A.
7. Lay the boxes on top of wing and tie the longs. to the

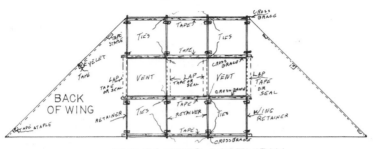

FIG. 14 WING ASSEMBLY

retainers every 3 or 4 inches. Leave 4" ties at the locations shown-FIG. 14-so the cross bracing can be tied
to the longs. with bow knots. DET. D.

8. Prepare 4 cross braces with hooks at the ends-DET. B.
Make them a length that puts a slight stretch to the
plastic. Set cross bracing in place with the top and bottom hooks through small holes in the tape and plastic,
DET. C. Those in the vents hook over the longs.

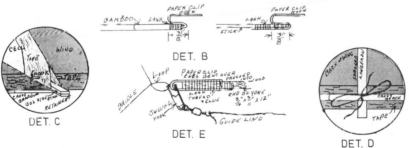

DET. B

DET. C

DET. E

DET. D

9. Tie braces to inboard longs-DET. D.
10. Make a wing spreader from 3' stakes slightly larger
in diameter than the Delta Wing Conyne; the span is
longer.
11. Tie a bridle of 40 lb. line-DET. A. Cross string from the
top cells to the bottom cells and looping as shown.
12. Trim a $\frac{3}{16}"$ x $\frac{3}{16}"$ stick to 12". Fix paper clips to ends. DET. E.

23

WINGED CONYNES

To fly as a single string kite, fasten the line to both loops. To fly as a stunt kite, fasten the lines to the loops and yoke as in DET. A. A pull on the left line causes a veer or loop to the right and vice versa. The entire foil warps when one line is shorter than the other. This makes the kite very effective in tacks to one side. It tacks like a lanteen sail, and its mirrored twin tacks beneath. The delta wing resembles a lanteen rig if the spreader is visualized as the mast and the wing stick as the leading edge spar.

Heavier wing stick can be substituted when flying in strong winds on two lines, and a heavy duty spreader in reserve would be prudent. When flying in light winds on a single line, the kite can be lightened by removing the cross braces-in part, or entirely.

This design may be varied by changing the size or the shape of the wing or the distance between the boxes. It can also be converted into a three string stunter with a third bridle tied to the bottom cells with a third line tied to it. Anchor this line to the ground so a step toward the kite brings it into play. The multitude is then amazed by a kite that not only rolls, dives, and tacks from side to side, but will also fly upside down, stop and hover in the middle of a screaming dive, land and take off again, either rightside up or upside down, or perform any other trick possible with a kite. Be prepared to repair some broken sticks while mastering these maneuvers, as the kite can be tricky when flying upside down with controls reversed.

Left to right- A Stub Wing Box-Same box with delta wing-Same wing on a Conyne box- The same Conyne box with the stub wings. It is done with two sets of wing spars, two delta wing spreaders, and bag ties. 1+1=4

STACKED DELTAS

This variation of the Delta Wing Conyne is not as complicated as it looks. It goes together nicely if the steps are taken one at a time. Since its appearance in Winter, 1977-78 issue of *Kite Lines*, it has won prizes in several major festivals. It can be covered with plastic or cloth and increasing its dimensions by 50% has proven practical.

The construction steps here differ from those in *Kite Lines* for reasons of simplicity, but the dimensions are practically the same.

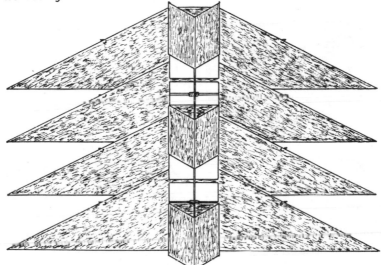

FIG. 15 STACKED DELTAS

MATERIALS

2 24" x 30" white kitchen can bags.
4 38"x $\frac{1}{8}$" dowels, sticks, bamboo, etc. to sandwich the wings to the box. See page 20, FIG. 11.
1 38"x $\frac{3}{16}$" x $\frac{1}{8}$" stick or $\frac{3}{16}$" dia. dowell for a keel.

Jennifer's Easter kite with its cerise,
plastic gift-wrap wings and yellow
boundary tape tails; the top kite to
a five year old.

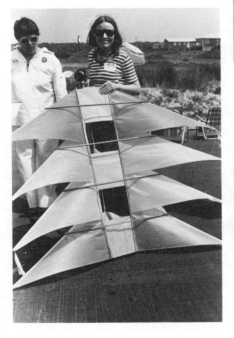

Top left-
A radiant Valerie Govig with AKA life
member, Aylene Goddard, and the top
kite at Nags Head, a rip-stop Stacked
Deltas. Its stirling behavior in tricky
conditions aided in the win.

Bottom-
Valerie surrounded by the prestigeous
competition that includes Bill Bigge,
the Rogallos, and the Marshalls.

Above two photos first appeared in Spring, 1979 KITE LINES, The International
Journal of Kiting. $12/year: PO Box 466, Randallstown, MD 21133-0466 USA ,
Used with permission. Photo by Ted Manekin.

8 24"x $\frac{1}{8}$"x $\frac{1}{8}$" sticks or $\frac{1}{8}$" or $\frac{3}{16}$" dia.dowels for the wing spars.

8 2' bamboo stakes approx. $\frac{3}{16}$" base diameter for spreaders and a length of $\frac{3}{8}$" dia. bamboo for the joiners at the centers.

Tape, glue, thread, eyelets, light twine, etc.

CONSTRUCTION

1. Lay out 4 wings and 2 cells on 2 24"x 30" bags.FIG.16. (Most bags have a bit of extra stock for two wings, but some brands are skimpy so do the best you can.
2. Tape or heat seal the hems on the cells and wings.
3. Stack the wings with 4"overlap(FIG. 17). Apply tape strips across the central section of the wing assembly. The wing section can be temporarily tacked down to board during this procedure to insure alignment. Fix retainer strips to back of wings with short lengths of tape.
4. Cut vents as shown. Fold laps over retainers to tape or heat seal. When heat sealing laps, slip cardboard between the wings so they are not sealed to one another outboard of the retainers.

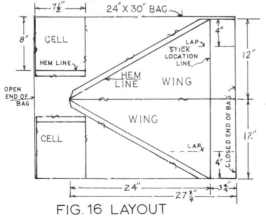

FIG. 16 LAYOUT

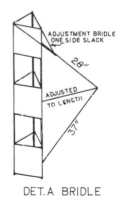

DET.A BRIDLE

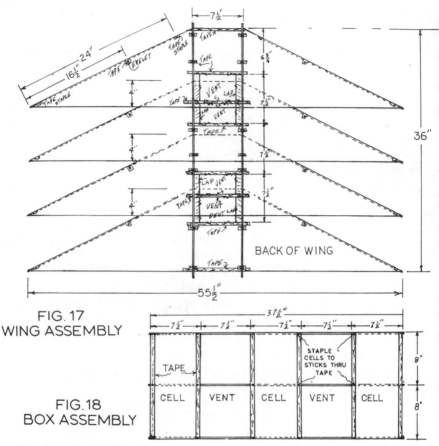

FIG. 17
WING ASSEMBLY

FIG. 18
BOX ASSEMBLY

5. Assemble the box section so the longerons and keel protrude $\frac{1}{4}$" from the bottom and top cells. FIG. 18.
6. Lay the box assembly on the wing and tie the sections together. See page 20, item 11.
7. Make 4 bamboo wing spreaders. See FIG. 8, pg. 17. These spreaders are for a smaller wing so substitute $\frac{3}{16}$" dia. stakes and follow the same procedure.
8. Tie a bridle as in DET. A. The strings running from the top leg to the ends of the longerons are correction bridles. Shorten one or the other to correct a lean.

28

Delta wings may be stacked on a Conyne box in many different ways. Here are a few hookups:

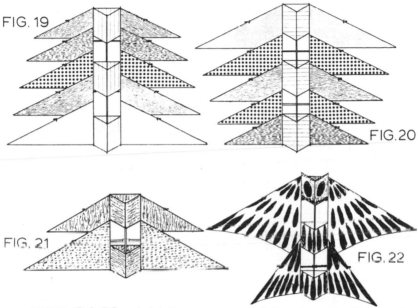

FIG. 19

FIG. 20

FIG. 21

FIG. 22

FIGS.19 & 20 might be compared to descending and ascending pentatonic scales. Increase the dimensions of the wings the same amount each step of the scale. If the smallest wing measures 9" by 18", it should lap $\frac{1}{3}$ of 9", or 3". The next wing should be 10" by 20" and overlap 3.33", the next, 11" by 22" and lap 3.66" etc. After the wings are assembled, measure the height and divide by five to determine the height of the cells. FIG.21 shows a 2-Stack and FIG.22 a Conynebird.

It is interesting to speculate whether the wing overlap creates a Venturi slot like that claimed for the Marconi kite, and, if so, does it improve performance? A test in a wind tunnel is the only way to find the answer.

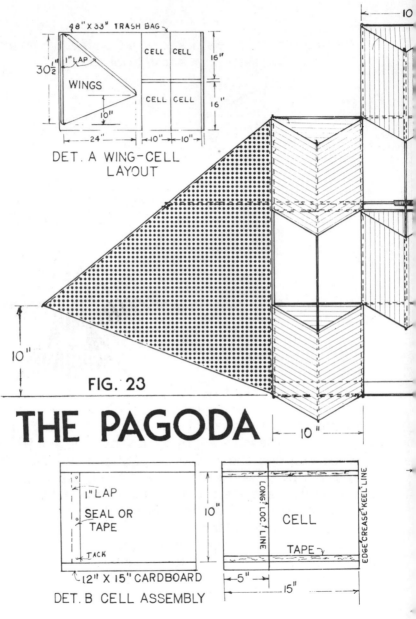

DET. A WING—CELL LAYOUT

48" X 33" TRASH BAG
1" LAP
WINGS
CELL CELL
CELL CELL
30½"
16"
16"
10"
24"
10" 10"

10

FIG. 23

10"

THE PAGODA

10"

DET. B CELL ASSEMBLY

1" LAP
SEAL OR TAPE
TACK
12" X 15" CARDBOARD
10"
LONG. LOC. LINE
EDGE CREASE KEEL LINE
CELL
TAPE
5"
15"

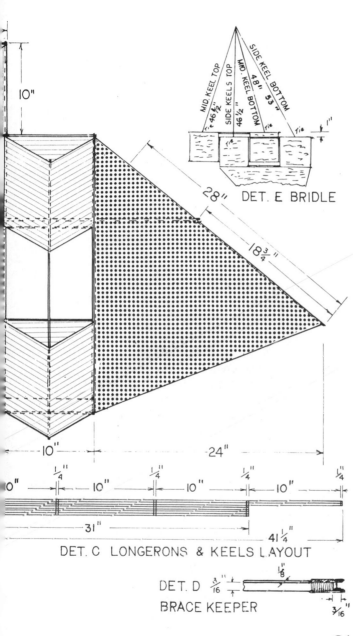

10"

SIDE KEEL BOTTOM
MID. KEEL TOP
MID. KEEL BOTTOM
SIDE KEELS TOP
48"   53"
46½"   49½"
Tie   Tie   1"

DET. E BRIDLE

28"

18¾"

10"   24"

0"   ¼"   10"   ¼"   10"   ¼"   10"   ¼"

31"   41¼"

DET. C LONGERONS & KEELS LAYOUT

DET. D 3/16"   1/8"
BRACE KEEPER   3/16"

THE PAGODA

"The Pagoda", for want of a better name, is another kite that is less difficult to build than its rather involved construction would lead you to believe. The kite has been built, flown, and has won prizes in this country and overseas. A kite this complicated deserves to stay around for awhile, so a covering of Ripstop or Tyvek might be used. However, trash bags also do well, so the directions specify that material, although other fabrics can follow the the same steps.

MATERIALS

2   33"x 4' trash bags.
2   $41\frac{1}{4}$"$x\frac{3}{16}$"$x\frac{3}{16}$" sticks.
5   31"$x\frac{3}{16}$"$x\frac{3}{16}$" sticks.
4   30"$x\frac{3}{16}$"$x\frac{1}{8}$" sticks.
2   21"$x\frac{3}{16}$"$x\frac{3}{16}$" sticks.   2 28"$x\frac{3}{16}$"$x\frac{3}{16}$"sticks.
2   31"strips of thin bamboo.
1   10"$x\frac{1}{8}$"$x\frac{3}{16}$" stick.
2   3' by $\frac{5}{16}$" dia. bamboo stakes.
1   4"$x\frac{1}{2}$"dia. bamboo stub.
Tape, light twine, eyelets, thread, glue, etc.

CONSTRUCTION

1. Lay out wings and cells on a trash bag-DET. A.
2. Cut out wings and cells as well as 2 cells from another bag.
3. Square a cardboard to 15"x12". Wrap a cell around it with the ends overlapping-DET. B. Tack the plastic and cardboard to a flat surface so the plastic is wrinkle free. Tape or heat seal so a cylinder is formed. Apply tape to the edges of the cell. Work the cell so the edge crease lies on the edge of the cardboard. Draw location lines 5" from the the other edge. The crease will locate on the center of the keel stick. The loc. lines will lie on the edges of the longerons.
4. Make 5 more identical cells.

32

Pagoda in Tyvek. Bottom- Its brother, S.S.T.

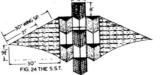

FIG. 24 THE S.S.T.

30" WING SP

21"

8"

8"

9'

30'

5. Mark loc. lines for the cells on longs. and keels.-DET. C.
6. Assemble the boxes. Start by stapling the bottom cell of the middle box to the $41\frac{1}{4}"$ longerons. Next staple the outer cells over and under this cell to these same longs.. Next staple the top cell of the middle box. Staple the the 31" longs. to the outer cells. Then staple the three keel sticks to the crease lines.
7. Seal the laps on the wings and insert the wing spars and the retainers using the same steps as in Delta Wing Box, page 16, FIGS. 6&7.
8. Tie the wings to the outer longs. every 4 inches as in the above.
9. Set the wing eyelets and make a bamboo spreader of 3' stakes tapering from approx. $\frac{5}{16}"$ to $\frac{3}{16}"$ diameter.
10. Tie 15 lb. monofilament between the outboard longs. at the bottom of the kite to maintain the width. This distance should be the same as that at other locations when the kite is extended or about $29\frac{1}{4}"$ between the inboard edges of the outboard longerons.
11. Prepare 4 $29\frac{1}{4}" \times \frac{3}{16}" \times \frac{1}{8}"$ cross braces. Lash $\frac{3}{4}"$ bamboo retainers to the ends-DET. D. The braces should be of a length to fully extend the kite but not pull at the stapled fabric.
12. Prepare a cross brace for the top cell with bamboo retainers as above. Wind a few turns of thread on the tips of the longs. and glue to form a stop to prevent the retainers from slipping off the ends. Do the same for the rest of the longeron tips where retainers might jump the track.
13. When the cross braces are installed, tie them to the inboard longs. with bag twists. Transport or storage of the kite is accomplished by removing the spreader and cross braces and rolling them in the kite. Wrap the bridle around the roll and stuff it into a paper tube

or a drapery rod box.

14. The bridle shrouds are anchored to the keels at mid-points of each cell. They are of a length that the keels lie in the same plane when the kite is extended. Tie and loop the middle shroud first, hang the unextended kite by the shroud loop and proceed with the other two shrouds - DET. E. Loop each shroud to the correct length and tie the loops together with a loop of strong twine or a snap swivel. If the kite leans to the right, shorten the top right or the bottom left stay and vice versa for a left lean.

Dimensions of the Pagoda may be enlarged, diminished, and the wing shape may be varied. Kites with cells as small as 6 inches or as large as 22 inches high have been successfully flown.

THE S.S.T.

This kite is a variation of the Pagoda featuring a high aspect wing and a third cell on the middle box. It is a consistent flyer and makes a graceful appearance aloft. Its construction is much the same as the Pagoda, but cells of smaller size call for lighter framing. Longs. and keels of $\frac{1}{8}$"x$\frac{3}{16}$" section should be sufficient. A third shroud ties to the middle box and a brace is fitted across the bottom of the bottom cell.

The flying kite - FIG.25 - has a covering of Tyvek, painted with acrylic paint. Imagine yellow, red, and blue in the different shaded areas to get the image. White plastic bags could be decorated with permanent ink felt pens for the same effect. Tyve , but especially polyethylene, are translucent and show up well with backlighting, the usual aspect of a high flyer. Better the kite, worse the squint.

35

Exotic beings using wing stacks: Top left, Ella from Egypt. She belly dances. Top right, the horrible Snarst from the Andromeda galaxy. Bottom: Thunderbird off and flying from his totem pole. See Chapter 5.

3
V'S AND W'S

Kit kites are one approach to kite building. The design and engineering, as well as the structural components, have been precalculated and preformed at the factory, and the builder puts the parts together like a scale model from a hobby shop. The factory can make or purchase mass produced plastic and metal parts and joiners not available to the average kiter, so some of the kites are are quite ingenuous and can be fun to assemble and fly.

THE WINGED "W"

This kite was inspired by the "W" kit kite that is remembered by some with affection, including Brummitt on page 67 of *KITES, A Golden Handbook Guide.* This little dandy must have been stable in strong winds but a bit frame heavy for light breezes. Putting wings on the "W" takes advantage of the ingenious design, but increases the effective lifting area without a corresponding increase in weight, and still keeps the stability.

Those who prefer a minimum of glueing, heat sealing, or sewing should like this kite. It is covered with a single piece of fabric and uses but four seams. The three dimensional contour is achieved through the framing.

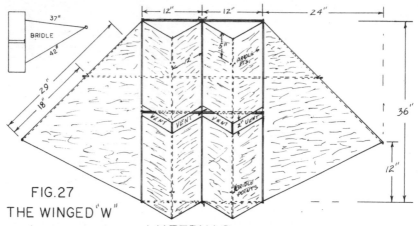

FIG.27
THE WINGED "W"

MATERIALS

1 oversize trash bag or a 3'x 8' piece of Tyvek, Ripstop, polyethylene, polyester, etc.

3 $36\frac{3}{4}"x\frac{3}{16}"x\frac{3}{16}"$ longerons.

2 $36"x\frac{3}{16}"x\frac{3}{16}"$ keels.

2 $29"x\frac{3}{16}"x\frac{3}{16}"$ wing spars.

3 $24"x\frac{3}{16}"x\frac{3}{16}"$ cross braces.

2 2' bamboo stakes of $\frac{1}{4}$" base dia. for spreader.
1 3" by $\frac{1}{2}$" dia. length of bamboo for spreader.
12 $\frac{3}{4}$" bamboo stubs for cross brace keepers.
tape, paper clips, bag twists, glue, thread, monofilament line - 10# test.

CONSTRUCTION

1. Lay out covering on a trash bag or other folded fabric and cut to plan-FIG. 28.
2. Apply tape as shown and seal wing slots.
3. Lay longs. on top of cover at outboard loc. lines and
center crease. Staple the fabric through the tape at
edges of the "W's" and 3 locations between. The longerons should protrude $\frac{3}{8}$" at the ends.
4. Staple the keels to the back of the kite so the tips lie
flush with the cover.

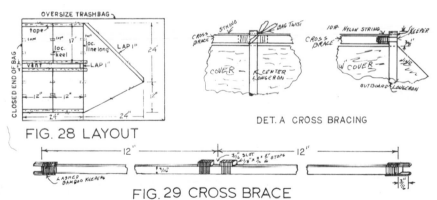

FIG. 28 LAYOUT

DET. A CROSS BRACING

FIG. 29 CROSS BRACE

5. Insert wing spars into slots and staple in place.
6. Prepare 3-24" cross braces with keepers at the ends
and stops to form a $\frac{3}{16}$" slot at the center-FIG.29.
7. Tie 10# test nylon line between the outboard longerons – monofilament will do–so the distance between
the inboard edges is approx. $\frac{1}{4}$" less than the cross

39

braces. One way to accomplish this is to lash the tips of the longs. with thread and glue, drill holes with a $\frac{1}{32}$" drill or a thin brad $\frac{1}{8}$" from the ends and in the plane of the wings. Thread the line through the three holes and knot the ends to the correct length-DET. A. Do at top, bottom, and in the vent.

8 . Set the cross braces in place at each end and in the vent. The braces fit in front of the middle longeron so the long. fits in the slots on the cross braces, the keeper on one end of the brace engages a long., the line is stretched, and the opposite keeper slips into place. The middle long is retained in the slots by bag ties.

9 . Prepare a wing spreader from bamboo stakes.

10. Make a bridle as in FIG. 27 Tie the shrouds as in the Twin Conyne Delta, DET. A, with the shrouds passing from the top cell on one side to the lower cell on the other. This makes for a guided kite.

This configuration can be exploited in several directions. The wing may be varied, or the delta wing abandoned for the traditional "Conyne" type. The "W" can be separated and a twin "V" emerges. A few of these suggestions are delineated here; the others the kitemaker may try on his own.

THE DOUBLE "V" DELTA

The building of this kite is much the same as the "W". Another longeron is needed, the fabric is 12" longer, the cross braces are 36" long and need a second slot, and the wing spreader is a foot longer and slightly sturdier for the longer span. Bridle the kite like the "W", with the shrouds crossed.

The proportions indicated in the plan are not final . The "V's" might be closer together, the keel angles may be increased or decreased, or the wing shape or area altered.

40

V'S AND W'S

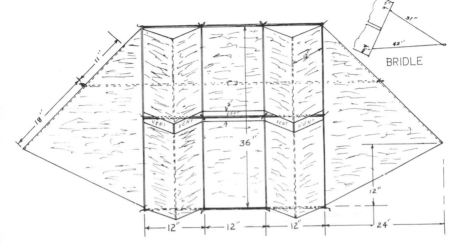

BRIDLE

FIG. 30 THE DOUBLE "V" DELTA

A Winged "W" in flight.   The Stubby "W" flies too.

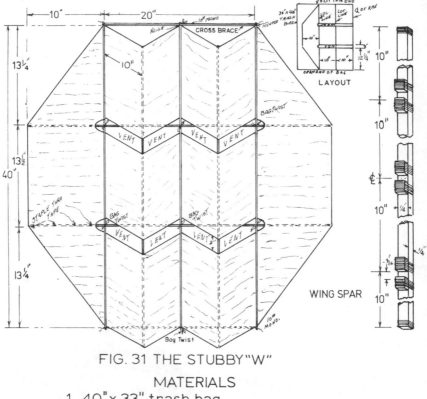

FIG. 31 THE STUBBY "W"

MATERIALS

1 40" x 33" trash bag.
2 40" x $\frac{3}{16}$" x $\frac{3}{16}$" keels. 3 40$\frac{3}{4}$" x $\frac{3}{16}$" x $\frac{3}{16}$" longs.
2 40" x $\frac{1}{4}$" x $\frac{1}{4}$" wing spars bamboo re-inforced.
2 20" x $\frac{3}{16}$" x $\frac{3}{16}$" end braces, tape, twine, bag twists, etc.

CONSTRUCTION

This kite is put together much like the Winged "W". The longs are held in alignment at the ends with cross braces with keepers at the ends, notches and bag ties at the centers, and mono. "springs" to keep the tension. Ties, notches, and tacks or staples keep the framing in place at the wing struts.

42

THE "VW"

If an idea works, it might as well be developed to the ultimate or even the ridiculous. Thus the "V W", so named for its prolifery of those shapes. Like the"W" kite(page 39), it needs but one piece of fabric to cover a whole section. The sections are then stapled to keel-longerons with a paper stapler. The rear longs of the first section serve as keels to the second which does the same for the third, etc. Covering can be plastic or cloth. Mine is Tyvec while H. B. Alexander of Charleston, SC and David Bowie from New Zealand? used cloth. These are the only "VW"s I know of so far.

But don't let the drawings scare you. Make up the four winged sections and weave them together with the keel-longs like a basket. The longs on the first-front section should be strong since the whole weight of the kite rests on them at launching. The cross braces can be light I made them of two $\frac{3}{16}$" strips of heavy grade bamboo fencing, thread and glue lashed face to face to straighten the warp. Two or three per section will do. Maintain the widths of the sections and the cells with monofilament "springs" (page 40, no.7) at the locations of the braces and with ties at the stops.

Wing spreaders should be strong for the rear sections due to their length. I used bamboo stakes tapering from about $\frac{1}{2}$" to $\frac{1}{4}$". Support them with loops tied to the longs as shown to prevent excessive bending or flopping. Bridle shrouds are 40# test and can be set to either a steep or shallow attack. I prefer the latter. This kite pulls like crazy. Use 200# line for the sake of hands and fingers if for no other reason.

1. The article also mentioned Tasmania.

V'S AND W'S

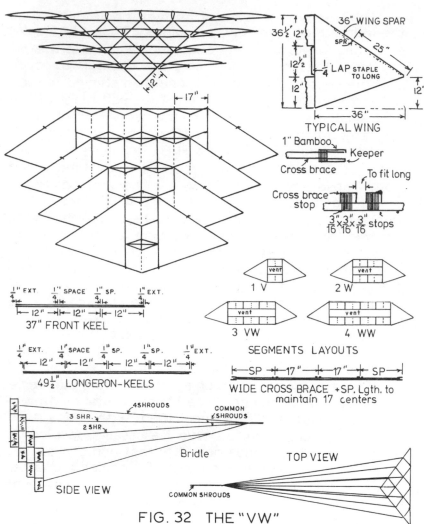

36½" 12"

36" WING SPAR

SPR

25"

¼ LAP STAPLE TO LONG

12½"

12"

12"

36"

TYPICAL WING

1" Bamboo

Keeper

Cross brace

To fit long

Cross brace stop

3/16" × 3/16" × 3/16" stops

¼" EXT. 1" SPACE ¼" SP. ¼" EXT.

12"   12"   12"

37" FRONT KEEL

¼" EXT. ¼" SPACE ¼" SP. ¼" SP. ¼" EXT.

12"   12"   12"   12"

49½" LONGERON-KEELS

vent
1 V

vent
2 W

vent
3 VW

vent
4 WW

SEGMENTS LAYOUTS

SP   17"   17"   SP

WIDE CROSS BRACE +SP. Lgth. to maintain 17 centers

4 SHROUDS

3 SHR.

2 SHR.

COMMON SHROUDS

Bridle

TOP VIEW

SIDE VIEW

COMMON SHROUDS

FIG. 32 THE "VW"

THE STACKED V-OWL

Since the Stacked Deltas came out in *Kite Lines* in the winter of 78, it has gone through many mutations at this address and others throughout the kite world. It became a winged sled here and then the multiplaned "VW". Then Joel Scholz appeared with a kite with its three delta wings of increasing size peeping over one another. The kite did keep the "VW" decoration scheme.

But it took the Professor, H.B. Alexander, to come up with a howler. His is of cloth, but making one of Tyvek is not difficult, and with dimensions drastically reduced (about 50%), plastic trash or store bags do well. So here is H.B.'s sketch and ingenuous schematic

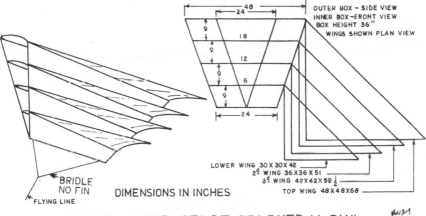

OUTER BOX – SIDE VIEW
INNER BOX – FRONT VIEW
BOX HEIGHT 36"
WINGS SHOWN PLAN VIEW

LOWER WING 30 X 30 X 42
2d WING 36 X 36 X 51
3d WING 42 X 42 X 59½
TOP WING 48 X 48 X 68

BRIDLE
NO FIN
FLYING LINE

DIMENSIONS IN INCHES

FIG. 33 FOUR STAGE STACKED V-OWL

Do not panic or be perturbed with the Professor for his schematic that combines three views into one drawing. He derives an innocent amusement from one losing one's bat swinging at his knuckle ball. Besides, he is still digging out from under Hugo and hasn't much

45

time. It may help to visualize the top wing section as shown here: Longs ac and bd are the top line of the outer box, ab and cd are the top line of the inner box. They fit in place if you visualize the wing section hanging in space through the top line. The $3^{\underline{d}}$ wing section has a similar look with 42" longs and an 18" center; and so forth for the $2^{\underline{d}}$ and lower wings. The 9" spaces also show the dimensions of the panels that join the wing sections. With all these parts put together, the kite in the sketch should appear.

To make the kite of Tyvek, constuct the V: Glue the tabs to form slots for $\frac{1}{8}$ in. bamboo strips. Construct the lower wing section and tape $\frac{3}{16}"\times\frac{3}{16}"$ longs to the back. Construct two panels: Glue the tabs and slip in the bamboos. Join the V, wing, and panels together in a sandwich by sewing through the Tyvek, around the long and panel bamboo strips with strong cotton twine, and tie a well cinched knot every 3 in. Add a pair of extra ties at the ends. Continue in like manner with panels and wings until the kite is assembled. Slip a 2 ft.x $\frac{1}{4}$ inch dowel or $\frac{1}{4}"\times\frac{1}{4}"$ keel stick into the V and tie in place. Fix each knot with a dab of glue.

Prepare wing spars and spreaders with dimensions and locations typical for each wing section. Cut holes in the panels to accommodate the bottom three spreaders and tie loops from the longs on the top wings to support the long spreaders. Tie a bridle of 200# line and a flying line of the same test.

Pick a day with steady winds in the 8 to 15 mph. range to try this kite. If your first trial is at 20 mph.

46

you might lose an arm. You don't expect a kite with delta wings 4 ft. high by 10 ft. wide to pull that hard, nor would you expect it from the kites in train . Bernoulli or Venturi or both must be in there some place. With this format wings may be added at will, and the Proffessor has added one with the use of clothing hooks so the kite's size can be varied.

But let's hear the rest of the story. While the kite flies great in a steady wind, it comes down fast during a lull. It won't float around like a single wing delta and will not respond to tugs or taking in line but answers only to a sprint downfield. So save this one for your day at the beach where you can vie with parafoils in weight lifting. So the following is a valley version for off again on again winds :

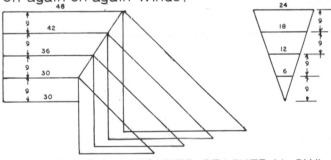

FIG. 34   MODIFIED STACKED V OWL

The dimensions and shapes for this version are similar to H.B.'s except for the connecting panels and the keel.

The squared panels put more area of the wings in a position where the wind can reach them as the kite changes from its almost vertical flight and flat angle of attack to an aspect more against the wind . Venturi has taken a recess and the less wind shadow the better . The increase in the keel length allows the bridle tie

47

to be raised to match the shift in the center of effort. While still not as buoyant as a single wing, the change has helped, but the symmetry of H.B's design has been compromised. Wings cannot be added here at will.

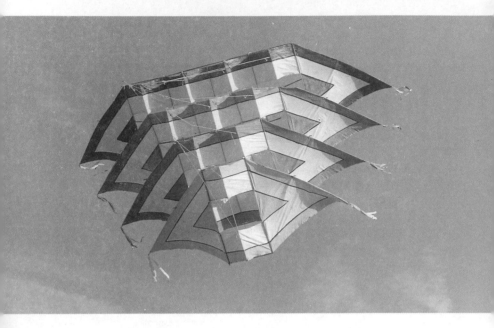

Der Volkswagon (V W)

A modified 4 stage V-Owl

4
WINGS AND SLEDS

Since sleds have come on the scene, there has been no reason for doing without a kite except lack of desire or lack of know-how. A couple of sticks and a plastic bag or just a paper grocery bag and you're in business. Tape and a bit of string and you have a kite. There seems to to be as many sled designs as experimenting kiters, and they are a great first kite for a toddler, since they are fairly rugged and very replacable.

MULTIPLE SLEDS

I gave Tom Caldwell a plastic grocery bag sled as a going home present from our golden wedding anniversary. He took it home and for the first time suceeded in lofting a kite from his front yard in San Mateo which lies on the lee side of a big hill- great for down drafts. He then bridled two sleds side by side and got them to fly and thus was the start of my quest.

I use the laterally vented sled as developed by Paul Sroka (Kite Tales; Autumn, 75). It's the best I have tried. Straight matchstick bamboo or round tubes from cheap plastic blinds do for longs. $\frac{3}{4}$" masking tape holds the longs to the kite pretty well if correctly applied (see ↓).

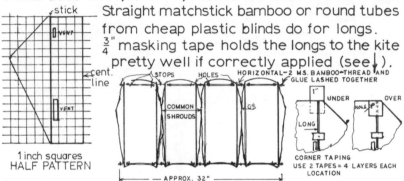

Double tape the fin corners as above. Punch holes for shrouds- no eyelet needed-wee kites-and tie 8 to 10 foot shrouds-wide kite. Use light cotton so this slip - knot will hold: FIN You will need this to get the kite adjusted. Five shrouds in all. Tom taped the fins of adjoining sleds together like this on his twins so I followed suit although they might not be needed. Thread the horizontals, set the stops → Mine flies well, 5 in a row too as well as 2 rows of 5 and 3 rows of 6. But you can figure those out from the pictures. Go for it !!!

50

THE SANDWICH SLED DELTA

Adding a wing to a sled seems the thing to do of late, so here is a kite that complies with the trend. It is easy to build, requires simple tools and ordinary skills, and requires no exotic materials.

Note: If dowels are used for framing, use string ties through tape for fastening. Stapling into a dowel is difficult. Use $\frac{1}{8}$" dia. dowels for longs., $\frac{3}{16}$" dia. dowels for wing spars.

MATERIALS

2   24" x 30" kitchen trash bags.
4   $24\frac{1}{2}$" x $\frac{3}{16}$" x $\frac{3}{32}$" spruce or pine sticks.
2   $30\frac{1}{2}$" x $\frac{1}{8}$" x $\frac{1}{8}$" sticks
2   2' x $\frac{1}{8}$" to $\frac{3}{16}$" bamboo support stakes and a 2" stub of bamboo approx. $\frac{3}{8}$" dia.
Tape, eyelets, paper clips, staples, etc.

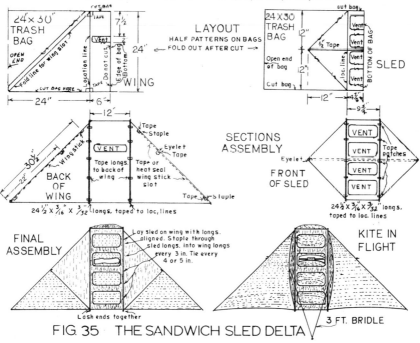

FIG. 35   THE SANDWICH SLED DELTA

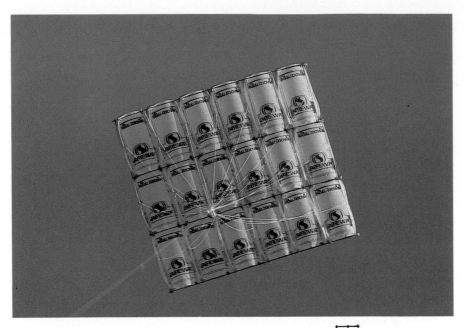

18 sleds in 3 rows. They fit on a matchstick bamboo frame: ⊞ The bridle has
21 ten+ foot shrouds. Look at it and think. It works. Great for light winds.

Left: T-Bird-2, a winner. Right, worm's eye view of a plastic store bag 2-Stack. Is
Venturi present?

CONSTRUCTION

1. Lay out wing and sled section. Cut and apply tape as shown. Tape or heat seal wing slots.
2. Set $\frac{3}{16}$" x $\frac{3}{32}$" x $24\frac{1}{2}$" longerons on the back of the wing and the front side of the sled and hold in place with short lengths of tape.
3. Turn the wing section on its back, place the sled on on the wing with the longs. and the sections aligned. Staple through the sled longs. into the wing longs. at 3"intervals with a paper stapler. (Thin paper staples will not split the sticks.) Sew through the fabric and around the longs. with a needle and light twine and tie every 4 inches. This will hold the sections together between the sandwiching longerons.
4. Slip the wing sticks into the slots, staple them in place through the tape patches and set the spreader and bridle eyelets.
5. Prepare a bamboo stake spreader from stakes $\frac{3}{16}$" dia. or less.
6. Tie a bridle as for any sled. A handy knot for sled bridles is the lariet loop knot. It starts with an overhand 3 in. up the string that is kept open as the end of the string is passed through the eyelet and back through

the open knot. Knot the end of the string and jam the knots together. To shorten, pull the end of the string through the slip knot, tie a new knot, and rejam. Sleds are very sensitive to bridle adjustment and this knot allows quick changes. To correct a right lean, shorten the right bridle leg, and vice versa.

This kite is a fine all-around flyer. It is light enough to float on the softest zephys but also has the stability to to stay up when the wind howls. It is remarkably tolerant to turbulence. Tie a separate line to each fin and it converts to a guided kite. Pull the left string to have the kite tack, dive, or loop to the right; the opposite for

THE STACKED DELTAS SLED

The construction of this kite uses the "sandwich" and puts a sled on a stack of delta wings. Make the wings the same as Stacked Deltas, except the midsection, which is 12" wide and is vented only at the spreaders.

MATERIALS

2 24" x 30" plastic bags.
1 33" x 40" plastic bag.
8 $\frac{1}{8}$" x $\frac{1}{8}$" x 24" wing spars.
4 $36\frac{1}{2}$" x $\frac{3}{16}$" x $\frac{3}{32}$" longerons.
8 $\frac{1}{8}$" to $\frac{3}{16}$" dia. by 2' long bamboo for spreaders.
4 2" by $\frac{1}{4}$" to $\frac{5}{16}$" dia. bamboo for spreaders.
tape, eyelets, string, etc.

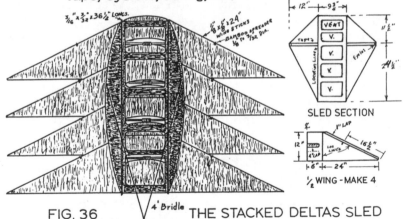

FIG. 36   4' Bridle   THE STACKED DELTAS SLED

CONSTRUCTION

1. Cut out 4 wings, seal wing spar slots, and stack wing section together as in Stacked Deltas-pg. 28.
   Tape longs. in place on back of wing section as in Sandwich Sled Delta.
2. Cut out and tape sled. Tape longs to sled.

3. Sandwich sections together with staples and ties-
   see Sandwich Sled Delta.
4. Set wing spars, eyelets, bridle, spreaders, etc.

The "Stack" elaborates the winged sled principle in fine style. It has looks, stability, range, and versitility- it doubles as a guided kite. Variations on the "Stack" are fun, and those shown with the "Conyne" center work as well with the sled.

Making a plastic sandwich.

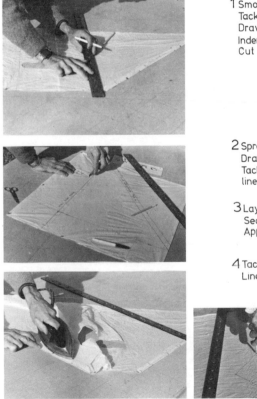

1 Smooth bag to flat surface.
  Tack down with slight stretch.
  Draw shear and location lines.
  Indent loc. lines with ball point pen.
  Cut out wing on shear lines.

2 Spread out wing section.
  Draw loc. lines on other wing half.
  Tack wing slot loc. line to a straight
  line on the board.

3 Lay paper on wing slot hem.
  Seal hem with a hot iron.
  Apply duct tape to stress points.

4 Tack down a second bag.
  Line, cut, and tape sled section.

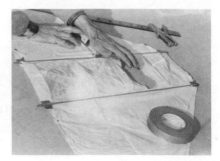

5 Tape longs to front of sled and back of wing.

6 Lay sled on wing with longs. aligned.
Staple long. pairs together every 4 inches.
Tie longs. together every 6 inches.

7 Insert wing spars into slots.
Staple through tape patches into wing spars .
Fix spreader and bridle eyelets.

8 Select pair of 2 ft bamboo stakes for spreader.
Glue-thread lash bamboo stub.
Ream stub to fit stakes.
Prepare spreader hooks.
Trim stakes to a length to spread kite.
Glue-thread lash tips of spreader stakes.

9 Tie 4 ft. bridle with slip knots

10 Spread kite.   11 Fly away.

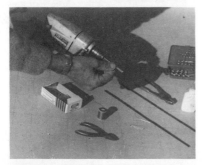

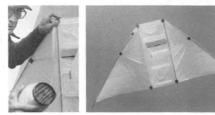

THE GOOGLE EYED SNARST

The Stacked Deltas doesn't really resemble any flying life forms on this planet, but a chance contact with some extra-terrestrial characters acquainted me with a creature from the Andromeda galaxy that utilizes the principle of overlapping wings. This odd species is widely despised for its antisocial lifestyle. However, it is intelligent, makes its own wings, talks by genetic radio, and is seeking help in curbing its Snarsty habits.

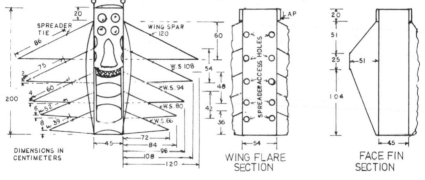

DIMENSIONS IN CENTIMETERS

WING FLARE SECTION

FACE FIN SECTION

If the above is confusing, look back to similar kites in this chapter. The kite is made of two sections; the front fin-face and the back wing-flare. These are joined at the long lines with a sewn long sleeve (in cloth) or by fixing each section to light longs with paper staples and then tieing the longs together in a sandwich. (See pg. 51) The overlap is figured from the bottom up. Wing one overlapps two by ⅓ of its altitude 36 cm or 12 cm. The next overlap 14 cm, next 16, etc.. The spreaders thread through holes in the flare. Sticks can be on the light side because of the narrow wings and the sled build. Decorations can be as snarsty as you please.

A LESSON IN CONSERVATION

This is not for those who have cut cloth following patterns or have done layout in metal fabrication. They know the tricks of material conservation. But those who are new to such activities might benefit from instruction in layout, so they wont start in the middle of the fabric and wonder afterward why they used so much material and then had so much scrap left over.

Even trash bags can be conserved, but a saving of a few cents might not generate enough of suspense to hold the reader's interest, so this kite is covered with Dupont Tyvek (Type 1422R), and a wee more savings are involved. The instructions also apply to Rip stop or any other fabric where both sides of the material are much the same in texture, color, or pattern.

MATERIALS

$2\frac{1}{2}$ yds. of Tyvek (Type 1422R), 56 in. wide.

2 $36\frac{1}{2}'' \times \frac{3}{16}'' \times \frac{3}{16}''$ wing spars.

2 $26\frac{1}{2}'' \times \frac{3}{16}'' \times \frac{3}{16}''$ tail spars.

4 $45\frac{1}{2}'' \times \frac{1}{8}'' \times \frac{3}{16}''$ longerons.

2 $2' \times \frac{1}{4}''$ dia. (at large ends) bamboo plant support stakes for wing spreader.

2 $2' \times \frac{3}{16}''$ dia. (at large ends) bamboo plant support stakes for tail spreader.

2 $3'' \times \frac{5}{8}''$ dia. bamboo stubs for spreader joints.

eyelets, thread, light string, 30# braided cord for bridle, jumbo paper clips, duct tape.

Acrylic paint - this kite is a natural for decoration.

LAYOUT

1. Cut patterns of wings, tails, and sled fins from paper or cardboard. Move them around on the material for the least waste. The sketch is one solution and there are probably better ways to do it. Notice that the longeron location lines run parallel or perpendicular to the edge of the fabric. Wheth-

er Tyvek has a warp or woof is doubtful, but to play it safely, lay it out as if it had.

2. Lay out the parts and cut.

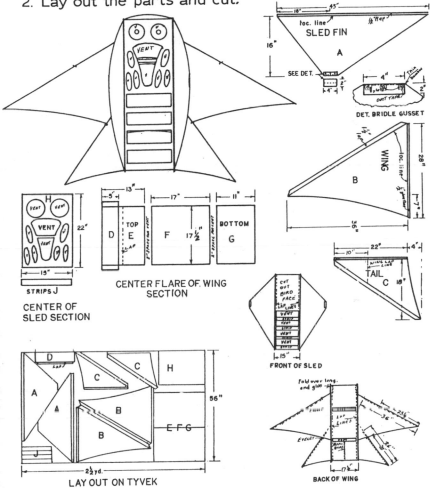

FIG. 37 THE THUNDERBIRD

ASSEMBLY

1. A handy way to assemble the kite is to draw parallel lines as shown on a plyboard or other surface.

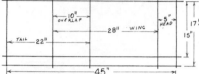 Draw lines at right angles $17\frac{1}{2}''$ at the several locations so the sections can be aligned. Lay the tails on the board with the loc. lines on the $17\frac{1}{2}''$ lines. Lay the wings on the tails and glue the pairs together at the flaps. Tack the loc. lines to the lines on the board.

2. Glue center flare panels to flaps as shown.
3. Tape longs. to loc. lines every 6", fold top tabs around longs., and glue. Glue wing and tail spar slots. Set the section aside.
4. Set sled fins to the 15" lines and glue the bird face strips to the flaps. Tape longs. to loc. lines on front of sled section.
5. Staple and tie the sections together as in Sandwich Sled Delta, insert the tail and wing spars and staple in place, set bridle and spreader eyelets, prepare spreaders for the tail and wing and spread the kite.
6. Tie a bridle with 4' shrouds of 30# test line.

DECORATION

1. Decorate the kite before assembling the parts, as is difficult to paint when it is fully assembled.
2. Artist's acrylic in tubes or jars adheres to Tyvek through sun, wind, hail, and pounding surf; and, since Tyvek is water resistant, the combination seems ideal. Thin the paint with water for wash effects; use almost as it comes from the tube for a glossy opaque look.
3. The Thunderbird is a mythical creature from Pa-

cific Northwest Indian lore and can be seen during ceremonies and atop totem poles, so decorations can be inspired by this.

4. For the benefit of overpassing aircraft (airplanes, balloons, flying saucers, etc.) and people atop lofty elevations (skyscrapers, precipices, etc.), it is a nice gesture to decorate the back side of the kite.

1 & 2- Laying out the Tyvek with the aid of corrugated paper patterns for the most efficient use of the material.

3- Putting the wing section together by tacking parts to lines on a grid drawn on a board. This aids in the alignment of the several parts.

61

THE EVOLUTION OF A BIRD

The Thunderbird won a beauty prize a few years back, but I saw some examples of the mythical bird that inspired me to give the theme another try. It worked again; another prize. Of course, these birds are usually perched atop totem poles.

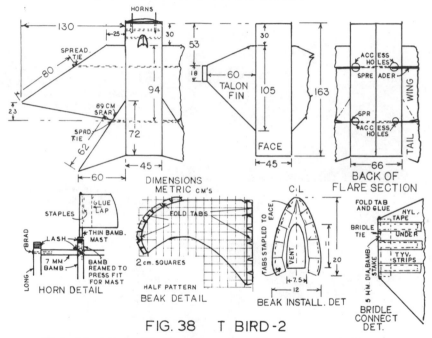

FIG. 38   T BIRD-2

This bird is built the same as No.1 except for some changes in shapes in wing and fin. The face is a sheet of Tyvek with no vents so the kite's center section is like a parafoil cell. Put a bow in the longerons and the likeness is heightened. The beak is made from stiff Tyvek as in det. Fold a 44 x 26 cm piece, draw the beak and tabs, and cut. Spread at the fold, fold the tabs under and you should have a beak ready to install on the face. Draw the wishbones on the face and cut out the vent. Staple the curve tabs together. A few staples on and near the fold installed from the top creats a ridge. Next staple the back tabs to the face. A pistol grip stapler is good here. Some staples can be placed exactly on the tab fold line. The beak can be held in shape with a bamboo cross brace (see the beak vent) with a second stake fastened: A brad through the cross brace into the beak prop which is cut just long enough to keep full extension on the curve and is in turn held in place with another brad pushed through the Tyvek into the stake's end keeps the beak extended. The width is maintained with a 2 x 2 x 10 cm styrofoam girder resting on the stake and held in place with brads through the Tyvek.

Ream the horn mast standards to create press fit sockets for the masts. Scrape or file flat areas on the standards and the cross brace at the joints. Lash them in place with thread and glue. The standards can be kept upright with another cross brace or a string inside the cell holding them against the back of the face.

While these aerodynamical noncontributing frills do little to help it fly, they don't hurt much either. A spare ear can be helpful, and an occasional beak lift keeps it fierce and proud. Someone should design a removable one (secured with clips?) so the kite can be rolled up.

"T"-BIRD-3

This mutation was created to convince sea gulls, Homo sapiens, and canines that a giant bird is in their neighbor- hood. It succeeds with the first two and even draws yips and growls from the third while at low altitudes. This is a result of a most authentic wing flap much resembling a hawk hovering over a chicken coop.

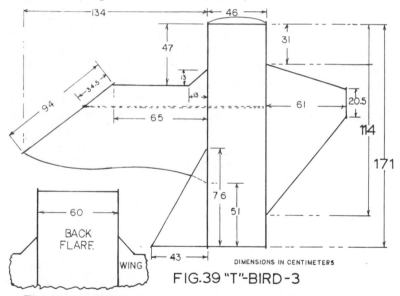

FIG.39 "T"-BIRD-3

The wing flap is caused by the shape and length of the wings and the connection points of the flexible spreader, The spreader is passed through loops tied at the longs so its gyrations do not damage the passage holes through the flare. Otherwise it is much the same as"T" Bird 2.

It does its best act in winds from 5 to 10 m.p.h..

A KITE WITH LONGITUDINAL CONCAVITY

The original patent of a sled type kite incorporated a concave curve along the longerons which is not seen on on the so-called Scott sled. The kite's aspect to the wind was similar to that of a boat sail. This accomplished an increase in lift and stability.

The author discovered this phenomenon independently and wrote about it in *KITE TALES*, Nov . 1976, "Putting Longitudinal Curve in a Sled". This kite flew high and true during a whole kite fly, enduring winds that gusted to forty miles per hour. Its only problem occured during retrieval, when a sudden gust, a stall aspect, and a short line combined to tear out a bridle grommet and snap the sticks.

Building a curve into the afore-mentioned sled was a bit complicated, and there was that annoying resistance of sleds to material changes. Subsequent kites of this type were not so successful. The kite in FIG. 35 can be easily curved on the longerons, and, since the kite's area is more wing than sled, choice of covering materials is not so critical.

This kite is put together much the same as the Stacked Delta Sled; the wing and sled sections are sandwiched between longerons that are stapled and tied together. However, there is a set of fins for each set of wings to facilitate the curving. The curve in the longerons is fashioned with a combination of bow strings and spacers. The strings should be snug with the spacers determining the degree of curvature. The exact amount of bow is best found through trial and error and may vary from kite to kite. Make several sets of spacers, from 2 to 4 inches long to find the optimum curve. The kite can be trimmed by adding bow to one side or the other, but bridle adjustment, as with any sled, is easier. An over

65

bow might have the kite trying an outside loop, although it behaves very well in an overfly; when the wind gets on top of the kite, it circles and flies back up, with a taut line during the entire maneuver.

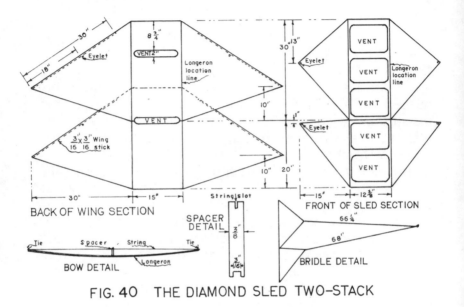

FIG. 40   THE DIAMOND SLED TWO–STACK

With the correct trim, the DIAMOND TWO-STACK is a spectacular performer. It seems to resent the line that restricts its aspirations and tries to escape, even as it circles in vertical flight. Other kites seem a bit bland after this one.

5
ODD BOXES

Kiters can celebrate the centennial of the Hargrave box kite within the next decade and ten years later pay homage to the Conyne pentahedron. And well we should, since these two gentlemen surely bequeathed a legacy to the kiting kind worth commemorating. If the preceding pages have not established this point, bear witness to the following, which should prove that the bequests are yet yielding treasure.

THE BRISTOL BOX

Dan Leigh, an English kite designer and builder, sent a rough sketch of a commercial "box kite" sporting odd shaped cells to H.B. Alexander of Charleston, SC. Dan expressed reservations about the kite but did admit to seeing one flying high over Bristol, England during a high wind. H.B. made some changes and sent them along. This is a light wind Silicone Valley version of the Bristol Box Delta.

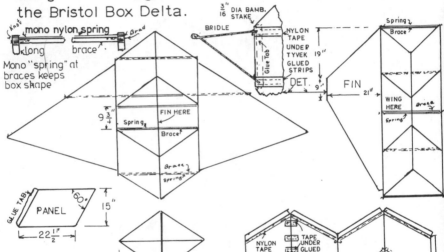

FIG. 41   BRISTOL BOX DELTA

This kite involved several experiments. The first was getting the box to accommodate a big wing. We catamaran sailors tend toward overrigging. An unruly

Bristol Box Delta in house wrap Tyvek

"Sergeant" in basic plastic bag

yaw was quelled with the big fin. Next, the covering chosen was Housewrap Tyvek; it was free. After the third kite and many disasters, reasons for not reccommending the 1000 type Tyvek for kites were dearly learned. It doesn't drape as well and tears easier than T14. It cracks at stress points (joints, wing spar ends , etc.). It sports a recurring red logo every few feet. It is harder to glue than type 14 and sews poorly. But it also has a pair of sterling virtues. It paints well on both sides and is more available for the thrifty kiter.

The following minimize the deficiencies:

1. Making a big kite eases the drape problem. This kite is over 10 feet wide.
2. Use Nylon strapping tape under Tyvek strips (type 14 if available) at stress points. See det., FIG. 41.
3. Work around the logo, put it on the back or paint over it in red or get a job in Dupont's p.r. dept.
4. Make big glue tabs, use lots of glue and pressure.

This kite turned out well but these variations from H. B. Alexander could prove better :

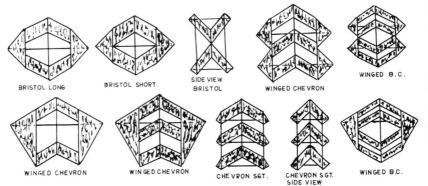

BRISTOL LONG   BRISTOL SHORT   SIDE VIEW BRISTOL   WINGED CHEVRON   WINGED B.C.

WINGED CHEVRON   WINGED CHEVRON   CHEVRON SGT.   CHEVRON SGT. SIDE VIEW   WINGED B.C.

The good Professor's obsession with this shape can be easily explained. He is expert at making cloth kites and finds construction shortcuts that he shares through articles in the kite periodicals. In the Bristol he has found a mother lode. The following shows some of his wiles:

To quote H.B., "The things (Bristol box cells) are so easy to make that I went hog wild with them for awhile." This fevered affair may be condoned in the following explanation:

1. Determine the sweepback angle. This is constant for all corners of a given cell but may vary from kite to kite or even cell to cell. Cut cardboard pattern, fin size.

2. Prepare a strip of material the length of the cell. Fins at the corners use up length so experiment with a strip of paper cut to scale and a paper stapler to set the seams so to get the size and shape desired.

3. Fold the strip of material in half and seam the end to form a typical Hargrave cell as below. Fix the seams as shown- sew cloth, sew or glue Tyvek with reinforcement, heat seal and tape plastic. Pen centerlines on each side.

4. Refold cell at centerlines and seam. Voilà! A four finned cell.

Three cells make Sergeant at the right. Another cell and a two cell inversion make a B.C., page 69. Trim the outboard fins and various type wings can be sewn or sandwiched on. The lengths of vertical and horizontal spreaders are optional so the box may have a square or rhombus shape.

This is a new breed.

Thanks, H.B. Alexander.

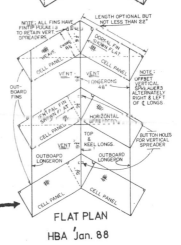

FIG.42-CHEVRON BOX→
"SERGEANT"

FLAT PLAN

HBA 'Jan. 88

NAVAL BARRAGE KITE

Gary Hinze lives down the way in San Jose. He is well known to kiters by his perceptive comments on the state of the art in *Kite Lines*. Gary never accepts the axioms of kiting as fact until he has tested them in the field and at his desk with his calculator. His kiting library is extensive and his kite collection museum grade.

He makes many types of kites, but his most interesting creations are probably his scale models of bigger kites. This barrage kite is an example of his ingenuity. Its scale is about 20 to 1 with the original and the construction details faithful to Harry Sauls, except for the abbreviated cross bracing and the bridle points. It flies good, but it is doubtful that it will down any airplanes.

MATERIALS

Tyvek, Type (1422-R) — strip $40\frac{1}{4}$" x approx. 8",

13   12" x $\frac{1}{16}$" x $\frac{1}{16}$" basswood sticks .

Length of flexible polyethylene tubing of dia. that fits snugly over basswood sticks.

Nylon thread, glue .

CONSTRUCTION

1. Cut Tyvek - Top cell, $40\frac{1}{4}$" x $2\frac{3}{4}$"
    Bottom cell, $24\frac{1}{4}$" x $2\frac{3}{4}$"
    Stabilizing fin, $4\frac{3}{4}$" x $6\frac{1}{8}$"
2. Draw loc. lines at 4" intervals on cells and $4\frac{1}{16}$" apart on the fins.
3. Crease all loc. lines.
4. Wrap cells around squared thin cardboards — 20" long for the top cell and 12" for the bottom cell.   Glue the ends together to form cells.
5. Slip 2 tubing cross brace holders as in det. on each of 2 12" longs so they will locate $1\frac{3}{8}$" from the top of the cell. The holders should be pushed together with the unattached sections pointing 90° from one another in

position to receive the cross braces. Lay the longs.
on the fin and glue them in place with the creases bi-
secting the face of each long., the fabric folds glued
together , and the assembly being exactly 4" wide.

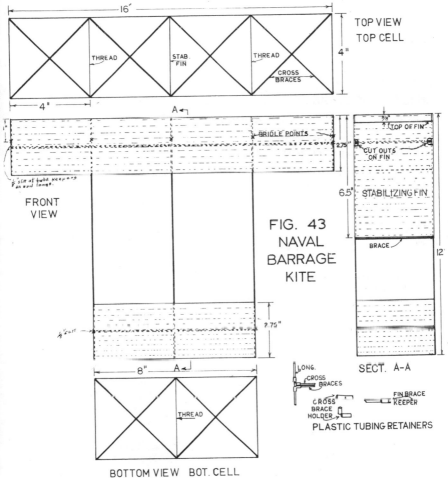

TOP VIEW
TOP CELL

THREAD STAB. FIN THREAD

CROSS BRACES

4"

FRONT VIEW

BRIDLE POINTS

2.75"

TOP OF FIN

CUT OUTS ON FIN

6.5" STABILIZING FIN

BRACE

12'

FIG. 43
NAVAL
BARRAGE
KITE

2.75"

8"

THREAD

BOTTOM VIEW   BOT. CELL

LONG.
CROSS BRACES

SECT. A-A

CROSS BRACE HOLDER

FIN BRACE KEEPER

PLASTIC TUBING RETAINERS

73

6. Prepare the $3\frac{7}{8}''$ fin brace and fit keepers to ends.

7. Slip tube cross brace holders for the bottom cell onto longs. and tie a thread between them to maintain a 4" space. Use the fin brace as a spacer and tie the thread at a slight stretch.

8. Slip 2 holders for the tops and single holders for the bottoms of 4 12" longs. Space the pairs with thread at the top as in step No. 7.

9. Slip single holders on each of the 4 outboard corner top cell longs.

10. Glue longs. and fin to loc. lines on insides of cells. The lines should bisect the inboard longs, but at the corners, the longs. fit right in the crease.   LONG ⌐ CREASE
   Make short slits in the Tyvek at the cross brace holders at the corners so they can come through the fabric and the crease will remain sharp and square.

11. The lengths of the cross braces can best be obtained by drawing the top view of the cells with the square tops of the longs. showing in actual size. Take the measurement for one brace from the drawing, set it in place and cut the other of the pair of a length that both braces have a slight flex. Continue in like manner at all locations. Set in the fin brace.

12. Tie thread shrouds from the bridle points to come together about 12" from the kite.
   Treat it gently; it is a dainty thing.

Gary Hinze's Naval Barrage Kite.

An unCorner Kite in basic brown & white trash bag after H.B. Alexander.

AN unCORNER KITE

Professor H.B. Alexander of Citadel University has designed this variation of the Rogallo corner kite. However, it is no longer an inside out corner box but has become an inside out Hargrave box with dihedral. This kite is experimental with adjustments galore. Do not attempt it if you are short on time or patience.

MATERIALS

4 3' x $\frac{3}{16}$" x $\frac{3}{16}$" wing spars.
1 4' x $\frac{1}{4}$" x $\frac{1}{4}$" spine.
2 24" x 30" kitchen trash bags.

vent or mylar tape, glue, thread, brads, etc.

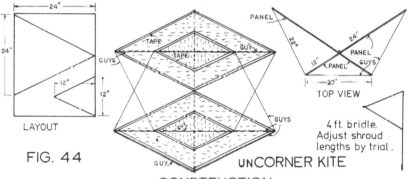

LAYOUT

FIG. 44

TOP VIEW

4 ft. bridle.
Adjust shroud
lengths by trial.

unCORNER KITE

CONSTRUCTION

1. Lay out and cut wing panels as shown.
2. Tape wing edges so tape folds over the edges.
3. Lash tips of spars and bottom tip of spine.
4. Drill $\frac{1}{16}$" holes at spar lashing locations and thread a short length of light line through each hole. Tie into small loops.
5. Assemble kite as shown with the guy strings tied to the loops at the spar tips. Tie slip knots in the guys so they can be adjusted during trial flights. Lead edges of the panels should be taut and smooth for efficient performance. Depending on the covering used, guy adjustments may vary from those shown.

6

AN ETHNIC KITE

A youth spent in the Ponderosa Pine country probably set the direction of the kites in this book. Frames for our kites were of the native wood split from boxes-wooden boxes were plentiful in the twenties-or from the planing mill resaw's edgings. However, an experience at the same time in a different direction also left an impression. A group of young Filipinos employed in the lumber mill on work visas lived in segregated dormitories a block away from our house. For entertainment they sang to guitars and ukuleles and flew beautiful native kites—

> —Multiple, tropical, fringed with a feathery flame,
> Like birds of paradise.—   E. A. Robinson, <u>Uncle Ananias</u>

that flew as good as they looked. Although this kiter's experience has been in other directions, admiration for these loveliest of ethnic kites has remained undiminished.

It is an uncommon occurence these days to see Filipi - no kites flown by Filipinos, but Wayne Baldwin builds and flies them in Hawaii; *KITE TALES*, winter, 1976; The Do-It-Yourself Kiter, and Jerome Prager of the San Francisco Bay area is an outstanding exponent of the art. Jerome, as a lad in the Phillipines, learned to make the kites from bamboo, but he builds "naturalized" versions here, with spruce framing. The kite described in the following is but one of many configurations that can be built around the Filipino dihedral wing. Construction of this kite requires subtle adjustments that can only be learned by experience, so the plans may be considered as basic guidelines.

1. MALAYSIAN HALF-MOON KITE
MATERIALS
2 $48" \times \frac{1}{8}" \times \frac{3}{8}"$ spruce wing sticks
1 $29" \times \frac{1}{4}" \times \frac{3}{8}"$ spruce spine
2 $36" \times \frac{1}{8}" \times \frac{1}{4}"$ spruce "moon" sticks
Tyvek, Type (1422-R) for cover
Strong thread, glue, acrylic paint, etc.
CONSTRUCTION
1. Select the wing and moon spars carefully for equal and even bend. Take your bathroom scales with you when you buy the sticks. See page 14, No.2.

2. Taper 12" of the ends of the wing spars.(Test for flex with the bathroom scales while tapering.
3. Tie mid-points of the wing spars to spine as indicated.
4. Lash spar tips with thread and glue and drill holes approx. $\frac{3}{16}$" from the ends, just large enough to lace the tips together with strong thread.

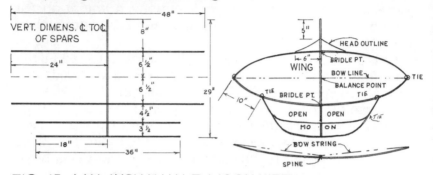

FIG. 45 MALAYSIAN HALF-MOON KITE

5. Lace the wing tips together. Tie a bow string from the wing tips to the spine, midway between the spars.
6 Tie the moon spars as shown and lash and drill tips.
7. Lace upper moon spar as shown. Lace lower spar to upper moon spar.
8. String the head outline as shown.
9. Cover with Tyvek.
10. Balance the kite between the head and the tail. Put your finger on the back of the spine about $\frac{1}{8}$ to $\frac{1}{4}$ in. below the bow line. The kite should balance equally from side to side and the head should point slightly down. Adjust the balance by adding weight to the top of the spine.
11. Tie a two leg bridle from the bridle points shown.

AN ETHNIC KITE

Jerome Prager gets by with a two leg bridle by carefully selecting and shaping spruce –he sometimes uses a tack board and water to warp the frame to shape–but a Filipino might rig a third bridle leg for trim correction. Wayne Baldwin advises a four leg bridle.

The third leg on A can be attached to either side of the spine depending on the trim needed. B can be adjusted either way. A similar bridle is used on Stacked Deltas.

1. Plan taken from KITE FLYER; The Bay Area Kite Flying News
   Instuctions by Jerome Prager and transcribed by Editor Leland Toy.

ENDANGERED SPECIES 1.
by
Neil Thorburn

Their tinted raiment decked the summer sky:
Six tailless tethered beauties like a show
Of dancers improvising in a row
Against an azure backdrop, on a high
Platform, wheron the low sun's mellow glow
Accents their paper pastels, as they fly
Controlled in free inverted puppetry
By swarthy masters fettered far below.

This antique artistry of tropic isle,
A paper sculpture on a bamboo frame,
Enhanced our heavens for a fleeting while,
But now in abdication sits the same
Old craftsman, while his grandson walks a mile
To buy a plastic pretense in his name.

1. This concerns Filipino kites. Whether it means the beautiful kites or the superb craftsmen who built them, is up to the reader. The extinction of either would be a pity.

79

7

KITE GEAR

The kite is the first step on the course and after that the line, but then the vistas widen. What is the line to be wound upon? This segment of kiting alone has generated a cottage industry, and, like any pastime, the possibilities for aids and gadgetry are boundless. (Has anyone provided designer kiting eyeshades yet?) Selected areas are to be discussed here, and a few embellishments and devises suggested for the kiter who enjoys making something from nothing much.

THE KITE LINE

This dissertation is not for the kiter who is confined by law or preference to altitudes of less than 500 feet where ease of handling and breaking strength are the main concerns. This is directed toward the adventurer who lusts after great heights and needs a lot of line to realize his aspirations.

If cost were no object, braided Dacron would be a good choice, and if personal safety were to be ignored, piano wire would do quite well as it did for the U.S.Weather Bureau's early experiments.(They never lost a man, although lightning melted down wire, winches, and other sundry gear occasionally.)

A material that functions passing well as a kite tether is Nylon monofilament fishing line. It is readily available in strengths suitable for any kite except the very large and very small, it offers low wind friction, it is a nonconductor of electricity, and is about the cheapest line around when purchased on $\frac{1}{4}$ lb. spools at a cut rate hardware or drug store. A kite of average size can be sent out of sight for less than the price of a fast food lunch.

There are drawbacks to monofilament that should be considered. Here are some of them:
1. It is not the easiest line to handle. It can cut or burn as it runs through the fingers, but this is a danger with any thin strong line.
2. It is susceptible to heat, so friction from crossing kite lines etc. can melt it in a trice, but this is also true of other synthetics.
3. It abrades and scars easily and breaks with little encouragement at crimps and knots.
4. When under constant tension like a kite's pull, it assumes a permanent stretch. This is likely to occur at

thinnest parts of the line, so every time the line is stretched, it grows weaker.

5 . It has a tenacious memory for the shape of the reel or spool it has been wound upon, and, if care is not taken, it will tangle while lying on the ground.

6. Its elasticity and memory cause great pressures to build on any device it is wound upon. This can cause the device to implode, bend, collapse, or fail in some other spectacular fashion.

With such a discouraging dossier, how can the kiter commission such a tempermental agent? The following is intended to assist:

1. Use gloves or a reel or learn how to handle the line with the least pain possible. The author has used 15# test monofilament for kites up to 10 sq. ft. in area for several years with nary a scar to show. This is with a tin can winder and no gloves.

2. Avoid other kite lines, cables, etc.

3. Do not allow the line to be run over by cars or pulled across rough surfaces. Avoid crimps in the line and join it to swivels and other lines using only recommended knots.

4. Do not expect the line to last forever. No line does. Monofilament just lasts a little quicker.

5. If the line must be coiled on the ground, a lawn surface is best. Remove line only from the top of the coil, even if it means recoiling in order to retrieve the line. Keep your feet and other people's out of the coil.

6. Reels and other winding devices must be very rugged and should be of fairly large diameter.

For larger kites a good, reasonably priced line is Nyseine twine. It is sold in a variety of strengths, starting at 50# test and graduating to over 600#test. It also melts under heat and will collapse reels, but it handles better than its poor cousin monofilament and resists abrasion and other wear and tear. It is good line for guided kites and other flying at moderate altitude.

WINDING DEVICES

Here are some line winders for the make-it-yourself kiter. They are designed to withstand pressures of Nylon twines and do their jobs quite as well, or better than expensive commercial gear.

TIN CAN WINDER

This tool has more utility and sophistication than its humble origin and appearance would indicate. It is quite strong, is an efficient spinning reel, and will keep up to a geared reel if the user is adept. Its weight might seem a detriment while winding loose line, but the lift of the kite tranforms the weight into a asset. It is superb gear for light to moderate winds and for line from 10 to 20# test.

FISHING SWIVEL

DET. A
$\frac{3}{4}$" PLYWOOD PLUG

FIG. 46 TIN CAN WINDER

DIRECTIONS

1. Find a can to fit your hand of a tall type. For larger hands, tomato juice cans are about right.
2. Remove one end of the can.(Drink the tomato juice first.) Force a $\frac{3}{4}$" plywood plug to the closed end of

the can. Fill the can with corrugated paper circles, ✳ alternating the bias with each layer, gluing them together as they are forced in place. Force another plywood plug into the open end and tack in place.

3. Winding the line correctly is of utmost importance. Start with a few circular turns and then start crisscrossing. After 30 or 40 turns, shift the can to a different position so the next series of turns are farther around the can. Continue in this manner so the line is wound evenly and tightly. Tie a swivel to the end of the line.

With careful winding and a little discipline, the "Can" does yoeman service. Each turn takes in from 13 to 15 inches, and it dispenses line at any rate desired. Improper winding, however, can mean a nest of snarls.

✳ Polyurethane pour foam will work too-easy but expensive.

LINE WINDING DEVICES

Left to right: The stick-oldest but handy. Trick is in the winding. Wrist action and constant turning of the stick helps build the shoulders. Use large dia. stick The can-Good for light lines and small kites. A winder-Like the plastic commercial variety. It is rugged and holds lots of line. Far right-A reel for a lot of line and a hard pulling kite.

REELS

As kites get larger and more line is dispensed, winding by hand becomes a chore. Commercial gear is not much unless one does not mind a substantial outlay on a deep sea fishing reel. Here are some low budget plans for the make-it-yourself kiter.

These reels are designed to withstand the pressures of synthetic line used to loft hard pulling kites to high altitudes, but they need not be expensive nor require a machine shop to build. Materials and parts can be found in scrap heaps, salvage yards, and hardware stores. Dimensions vary with materials and the reel's purpose. Be sure there is clearance for your hand under the reel. The base here is 18". Clearance $2\frac{1}{4}"$. About right for a long arm and skinny hand. The disc's edges need smoothing with file and emery paper.

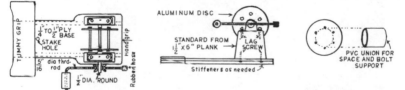

FIG. 47 BIG KITE REEL

Lenghts of pipe fitted over the bolts may be used to space instead of PVC. Clips slipped into grooves cut in the round are used to keep the reel centered. The bolts should be $\frac{3}{8}"$ in diameter or larger and the discs 6 to 8 inches.

The reel's gross weight of $5\frac{1}{2}$ lbs. might seem a bit much until a Bristol Box is straight over your head in a brisk breeze. Then it's a blessing. You can operate it standing, sitting, kneeling with foot, knee, or stake holding it down and then turn the handle into the standard for a brake. Speed or power can be gained by varying the length of the crank. Keep lock washers under the wing nuts. Will someone please design a simple drag brake for this rig?

The hand winder pictured has the space kept with VW valve guides from a trash bin. Countersunk bolts with screw heads keep the palm side smooth, and it is guaranteed to stand up to pressure and abuse.

POWER
REEL

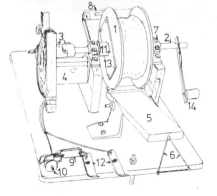

1. Disk brake reel.
2. ⅝" round shaft.
3. Slip clutch.
4. Wiper motor.
5. Drag & brake.
6. Rubber band regulators.
7. Bearings.
8. Guide.
9. Slow speed condenser.
10. Three way switch.
11. Plastic thrust bearing.
12. Connect tabs.
13. Riveted plate
14. Manual crank.

A POOR MAN'S POWER REEL

Manually rewinding line is not the high point of a kite flyer's day. Even a good hand reel is a chore after the first thousand feet. Here is a rig for the lazy frugal kiter. It eliminates the drugery of line retrieval with a small investment in time and money. Its power source, your car battery, might limit its field of operation, but you will, nev-er-the-less, be envied by your kiting buddies and mar-eled at by the gentiles, as you nonchalantly sip on a soft drink while your kite is returned to earth unassisted by human hands

CONSTRUCTION

The machine pictured is but one way to build the apparatus. Other approaches will vary according to the available materials and tools and also the skills of the builder.

The prime component of the device is the reel. It is made from a pair of automobile disk brakes. Your affable brake repairman tosses them in the scrap metal barrel when they are beyond repair. Acquire a pair of disks the size for your requirements. (The reel pictured is made of disks from a small sports car.) The hubs should be cylindrical. Bolt the hubs together (Existing lug holes do not allow for bolt heads and nuts so drill new holes.) Weight may be removed by turning the disks. $\frac{3}{16}$" is the limit on some brake machines. Otherwise, a thickness of $\frac{1}{8}$" would be sufficient.

Bolt or rivet flat bars across each face of the reel with countersunk heads on the inner surfaces of both disks. Drill a centered hole to receive a drive shaft of $\frac{5}{8}$" diameter in the flat bars.

Erect two standards for the shaft bearing housings and mount the shaft to the reel and bearings. The shaft

87

This kite and banner flew at grandson Greg Ray's wedding. The old kite man got a kiss from the beautiful Carrie. Wow!

can be secured to the reel by a weld or a $\frac{1}{4}$ in. threaded pin in the shaft stopped by self tapping screws in the reel. The latter allows for quick disassembly for changing reels etc. Plastic spools are adapted to act as spacers or thrust bearings to secure reel and axle in position. A crank is added for insurance.

The reel is turned by a windshield wiper motor that came equipped with an engage chuck that fit a $\frac{5}{8}$" shaft. A shallow hole drilled in the shaft receives the set screw from the chuck and the motor engages; loosen the set screw and the motor runs free and also the reel. The motor and shaft standards are made to accomodate this particular motor and reel. Wires run from the motor to metal tabs bolted to the edge of the base so current can be applied from the car battery via jumper cables.

Specifications of the reel include the following:
1. Capacity. $3\frac{1}{2}$ mi. of monofilament line-25# test.
2. Pulling power. 12 lbs.
3. Speed. 45 rpm or 3500 to 6500 f.p.h. depending on the amount of line wound on the reel.
4. Brake. Also acts as a drag to prevent overrun. It lets out line at a controlled rate–dispenses during gusts; holds in lulls–if rubber bands from the base are stretched to the end of the lever. Add bands as the wind freshens and vice versa.
5. Guide. Points reel toward the kite to keep the line from skipping the reel. It works in conjunction with castors under the front of the base.

This reel required a money outlay for 18 inches of $\frac{5}{8}$" steel round for the shaft, a pair of bearings, a secondhand windshield wiper motor, electric wire and clamps, and some bolts and nuts. The rest was reclaimed from scrap.

BANNERS

Kites are flown in some parts of the world to celebrate special events: a religious observance, or, for example, Boys' Festival in Japan. This charming custom can be adapted to our culture by adding a banner to a kite as a tail. A message in large letters on the banner will proclaim an occasion for blocks around; be it national holiday, family reunion, birthday, company picnic, or declaration of love.

A very visible banner can be made from 24" by 30" white kitchen trash bags. Slit the side seams of some bags so they unfold to 60 in. by 24 in. lengths of plastic. Overlap the ends of two bags an inch and heat seal as in FIG. 50   Continue adding bags in this manner until the desired length is attained. Seal an inch hem on each end of the banner.

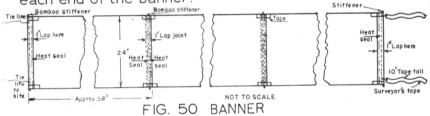

FIG. 50 BANNER

NOT TO SCALE

Print the message in large letters with large, permanent ink, felt pens. Slip light stiffeners into the hems and lap joints, and tie two tails to the bottom. Fix two tie lines to the top. All this will keep things rightside out and prevent twisting.   Taping the joints will lengthen banner life.

Ozz, the company photographer, caught this shot at the picnic. The banner provided a beacon enabling picnicers to find their section of the beach. The kite is a version of the Sandwich Sled Delta . It has a 7 ft. wing span and a lift area of $12\frac{1}{2}$ sq ft. It sports a sturdy spreader but weighs in at less than 8 oz. and stores in a 3 ft. tube.

PLASTIC PULLEYS

Occasionally the kiter may have need for pulleys for an auxiliary piece of equipment. If he happens to have a monofilament fishing line spool, a few simple tools, and some spare time, he should have his pulley made in less time than it would take to locate and purchase such an item downtown.

MATERIALS

$\frac{1}{4}$ or $\frac{1}{8}$ lb. mono. spool with $\frac{3}{8}$ in. dia. axle hole.
A $\frac{3}{8}$ in. dia. dowel, plastic glue

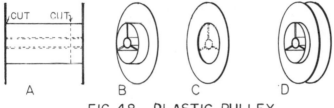

FIG. 48   PLASTIC PULLEY

CONSTRUCTION

1. Cut cylinder flush with flange at one end and $\frac{1}{2}$ to $\frac{1}{4}$ in. from the flange at the other. See (A).
2. Cut core from flange only end (C) and enlarge the opening until the cylinder of (B) fits through it with press fit. (D)
3. Remove (C), apply plastic glue to the cylinder, and press (C) into the desired position.
4. Insert a $\frac{3}{8}$ in. dowel or bolt into the axle hole and lubricate with a silicone or a dry lubricant.

These pulleys are light weight and strong enough for most of the uses a kiter might find. Plastic spools can be adapted to many uses, so, if you fly on monofilament fishing line, save the spools.

KITE GEAR

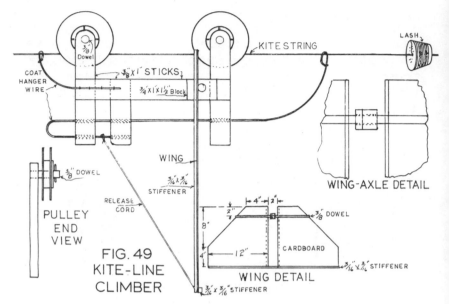

COAT
HANGER
WIRE

³⁄₈
Dowel

³⁄₈"×1" STICKS

³⁄₄"×1"×1½" Block

KITE STRING

LASH

WING

³⁄₁₆"×³⁄₁₆"
STIFFENER

WING-AXLE DETAIL

³⁄₈" DOWEL

RELEASE
CORD

PULLEY
END
VIEW

FIG. 49
KITE-LINE
CLIMBER

4"   2"

³⁄₈" DOWEL

2"

8'

CARDBOARD

4"

12"

³⁄₁₆" × ³⁄₁₆" STIFFENER

WING DETAIL

³⁄₁₆" × ³⁄₁₆" STIFFENER

This gadget is a poor man's version of Ray Biehler's climber in Wyatt Brummitt's, *Kites*. Monofilament fishing line spools are adapted to form pulleys, and the wing is made from stiffened cardboard. As the wing releases, the climber zooms down the line. Strong men blanch as it homes in on its kamikaze course. Disaster is avoided by keeping 20 or 30 feet of line coiled on the ground and releasing it at one time as the climber nears. The line will sag, and the missile will slow down.

A single pulley mounted on a board makes a handy tool for taking in a hard pulling kite. Send a helper to the kite with the kite line in the pulley to bring back either the kite or a length of line for easy winding. It is much easier on helpers than going hand over hand or trying to run the line under an arm, and it might prevent a broken kite line.

8

MODUS OPERANDI

Over half a century of intermittent building and flying
of kites (children and grandchildren are born and grow up
to interrupt or spur the process) should accumulate a
a residue of knowhow that can be passed along. The list-
ings following may at least give the reader something to
ponder. No scientific bases are claimed for the assump-
tions but only years of observations during trial and error kite building and flying, combined with a bit of emper-
ical reasoning.

BUILDING BIG

Big kites attract attention and are challenging to get up, to fly, and especially to hold down. They also are expensive, difficult to store and transport, and can be a hazard to the flyer, to property, and to the general public. The following observations are for those willing to bear the pain and go for the heavies.

Big kites generally require more wind than small kites. This is the effect of the disproportionate gain in weight over area. Area increases in two dimensions, i.e., length times breadth, while the frame and covering increase in three, length times breadth times thickness. This may be an oversimplified explanation, but it holds fairly true for everything that flies or floats. Extra weight means more drag which, in turn, adds strains to fabric, frame, line, and kiteflyer.

Therefore, it is advantageous to have a big kite light as possible so long as there is no sacrifice of structural integrity. Fly day may see your giant in the air rather than grounded during light winds, and, if winds blow hard, things can go better also.

Ways to shed weight include the following:

1. Utilize hollow framing–bamboo, aluminum tubing, box spars, etc.
2. Use multiple shrouds-the giants of Japan are examples.
3 Choose a design with multiple sections–the Pagoda is such a design with three keels, six boxes, etc.
4. Some framing needs little stiffness as they are well supported by fabric–longerons on sleds fall into this catagory.
5. Re-enforce frame members at stressful locations so they can be lighter in areas of less stress-delta wing spars and spreaders are amenable to this artifice.

94

6. Alter the design so lighter spars may be used for a given frontal area—this works well with delta wings.

WEIGHT SAVERS

The following are techniques for accomplishing some of the foregoing suggestions:

The Delta Wing Configuration—

The wings shown above have the same base and altitude dimensions. The first three have identical areas,

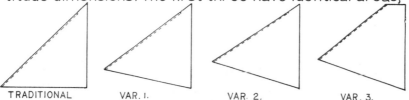

| TRADITIONAL | VAR. 1. | VAR. 2. | VAR. 3. |

while the fourth, as a result of its trapezoidal shape, has a greater area. The wing spars, on the other hand, grow successively shorter from left to right. The wing spars growing shorter may also be of smaller section. Weight is thus trimmed in two directions.

The Delta Wing Spar—

A delta wing spar may be strengthened for part of its length in the vicinity of the greatest stress. This may be accomplished by laminating to the inboard edge with a shorter stick and tapering it with a file or sandpaper after the glue dries. An aluluminum spar may be re-en-

INBOARD | LAMINATED RE-ENFORCEMENT WOOD SPAR SPREADER LOCATION

TUBE INSERT

ALUMINUM TUBING SPAR SPREADER LOC.

forced as shown by slipping the next smaller size tube inside the spar and fastening it in place with a pop rivet or metal screw. The spar can also be made up of three separate lengths of tubing in telescope connections as below. The larger diameter tube is in the stressful area.

95

SLIPIN JOINT ——| ————→ |←—| —— SLIPIN JOINT

ALUMINUM SPAR   └SPREADER LOCATION

The Delta Wing Spreader—

The delta Conynes and winged sleds need long strong spreaders which can add considerably to the weight of the kite. Since the greatest stresses occur at the mid-portion; the ends may be tapered like a longbow. Bamboo plant support stakes can be used for spreaders up 8 feet long, and rugs from the Orient still come with a sturdy bamboo stiffener in the roll. Importers in localities of high oriental population now sell the good stuff. In California, and other subtropical regions in this country, stands of bamboo can be found with poles 20 feet or longer, but this bamboo is not as sturdy as the imported varieties. Yet, it will suffice for spreaders 20 ft. long if two poles are joined in the center as in the plant support spreader (pg.17, FIG. 8).

Aluminum spreaders can be assembled in the same manner as wing spars with the middle third stiffened.

Note-Industrial harware outlets usually stock aluminum tubing in lengths to 12 feet and in outside diameters of $\frac{3}{8}$, $\frac{1}{2}$, $\frac{5}{8}$, $\frac{3}{4}$ in. etc. Since the wall thickness is .047 in., each diameter fits snugly into the next larger diameter tube. Very convenient.

The Conyne Core—

The triangular box that provides stability to several kites in this book does not contribute a great deal of lift per weight. It must be of sound structure since the forces on the airfoil concentrate at the keel. Shedding weight here should not be a casual procedure, but as a great part of the kite's weight is here, any legitimate reduction is money in the bank.

96

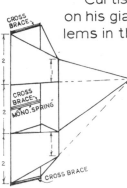

CROSS BRACE

CROSS BRACE
MONO.SPRING

CROSS BRACE

THE MARSHALL CUTAWAY

Curtis Marshall's innovation that he employs on his giant delta Conynes solves several problems in this area. He trims the fabric of the cells in the frontal panels at an angle. This shortens the keel by a third and also lessens the inward flex on the tips of the longerons and allows smaller section spars in both places. This is a benefit when building with aluminum tubing and fiber glass rod. While both are strong, both are limber.

Extra shrouds on the bridle (dotted lines) also make a lighter keel practical. Cross braces at the ends and the midpoint help to keep longeron flex under control. The midbrace should be held in place by a monofilament "spring" as described in Winged "W", pg.

The Spreader-Spar Connection–

The greatest stress on a delta wing spar is the spreader connection. This becomes more critical as dimensions increase. It can be relieved in ways other than beefing up the spar. The stress can be distributed over a greater segment of the spar by several methods. One way is with a cord, wire, or bracket anchored at two or more locations along the spar with the joint outside the wing.

LOOP

CORD

GROMMET

WIRE

ALUM. FLAT BAR BRACKET

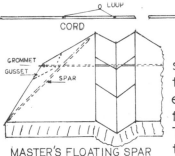

GROMMET
GUSSET

SPAR

MASTER'S FLOATING SPAR

Or the joint can be free of the spar completely as Carol Masters suggests. Here, the spreader connection is entirely in the fabric, while the spar floats free. The gusset and the grommet at the joint should be as well sewn

97

and whipped as those on a genoa foresail clew, since the forces on a big kite could be comparable. The rest of the design, including the backless Conyne box, might or might not adapt to a large kite, but the wing should do well. The spar could be lighter than in a conventional construction. Delta wing purists might decry the departure from the classic straight leading edge, but the paring of weight could make it worthwhile.

The Sled Core —

The longerons on the winged sleds require little rigidity in flight; they are entirely supported by the fabric and the opposing forces of the wings and the fins. They can be light and flexible. Slip aluminum flatbars or tubing into slots sewn between the wings and the sled, or use the sandwich construction with the fabric held between a pair of light aluminum flatbars pop riveted together. A good size plastic kite could be built with this method.

Kites of Parts—

Some kites lend themselves to enlargement because their total area is divided into several parts. As dimensions increase, no one part attains unmanagable proportions. The several "Stacks" of delta wings are examples of this.

A respectable "biggy" could be built by increasing the dimensions of the Diamond Sled Two Stack (FIG. 35, pg.65) by a multiple of 4. Each wing would have a width and a height of 10 feet. The kite would be 25 feet wide, 16 feet 8 inches high, and have an area of 268 square feet.

Wing spars could be of aluminum tubing or straight bamboo poles tapering from the top down. The spreaders could also be of aluminum or bamboo tapering from the center out. On a cloth kite a slot can be sewn with

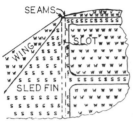

SEAMS

WING

SLOT

SLED FIN

LONGERON SLOT

two seams to hold the sections together in which a $\frac{1}{4}$" aluminum tube or $\frac{1}{16}$" or $\frac{1}{8}$" by $\frac{1}{2}$" flatbar is inserted. A plastic kite's longerons should be of the "sandwich" type in the plan with $\frac{1}{16}$" x $\frac{3}{8}$" aluminum flatbars and pop rivets taking the place of the wood strips and staples.

This kite has the advantage of compactness; a single wing kite of equal area would mean a wing span almost 40% longer with heavier requirements in both framing and covering.

Another kite that enlarges gracefully is the Pagoda. Its interlocking Conyne boxes make comparatively light longerons and keels practical as do the six shrouds. The design also accepts the "Marshal cutaway" for a further weight reduction.

The author built a "cheapy" with 22 inch trash bag cells; a typical bag is 66 inches in circumference, so a cell can be made by simply cutting off the top 22 inches of the bag. Each cell panel is a 22" x 22" square. The wings were of 3 mil polyethylene, the wing spars and spreaders were bamboo poles, and the keels and longs. were pine sticks sawn from scap edgings garnered from a cabinet shop. The kite was 18 feet wide and 7 feet 8 inches tall and flew easily and well on 100# test Nylon seine twine in winds from 5 to 20 miles per hour.

SUPER STICKS

Technology has produced some remarkable materials for modern expensive kites. They are one of the main reasons for the cost. But with a bit of perseverance and perspiration, the make-it-yourselfer can approach , equal, or excell the Nylon tubes or even the Dacron and carbon wonder spars. This will be especially noticeable in the weight to stiffness ratio. It utilizes the well worn process of bamboo lamination.

Materials needed are a straight grained edging of pine, larch, ash, et al, some heavy grade bamboo fence, and some white glue.

Tools include a saw to rip the edging into sticks, a jack plane with a well squared and sharpened blade, a length of light angle or channel, 8 or 9 steel spring or small C clamps, and all the kite clamps (clothes pins) you can raise.

1. Rip and trim edging to desired length and thickness allowing stock for planing. The bamboo laminate will add about $\frac{1}{8}"$ to the thickness of the stick so project.
2. Select a bamboo stake, split to fit stick but provide ample width to insure lamination. You slowly but surely learn to split bamboo as you proceed, and remember, the narrower the slat, the easier to to plane.
3. Plane the bamboo out (shiny) side first taking particular care with the joints. Plane other side in like manner. Sand the joints and other areas needed .
4. Align the stick to the edge of the channel and brush on a generous layer of glue. Clamp one end of the slat to the stick. Work down the stick with clamps and clothes pins. The bamboo may need flexing occasionally (crooked slat) to keep alignment, but

do not fret, as long as the stick remains even with the channel edge, all is well. The flexed bamboo adds stiffness (stressed concrete?) and the slat on on the other side can be set so the flex works in the opposite direction to equalize. Continue clamping until the slat is set. The stronger clamps should grip the joints and stress points while clothespins, about one per inch, hold down the rest.

5. Let glue dry, remove clamps, rough trim the excess bamboo with a knife and proceed to glue another slat to the other side of the stick as above.

6. After the glue has set, remove the clamps and trim the excess bamboo with plane and sandpaper until the spar is finished.

This may seem a lot of work for one kite stick, but if a few sticks and slats are prepared ahead of time, the laminating can be sandwiched between bouts with the lawnmower or TV programs. A few days may find a respectable number of spars on the rack. And these spars are worth the effort, especially on a kite as big as Thunderbird 2 that flies in winds that leave smaller kites in their carrying bags and also flies well in blows, all due to its Super Spars.

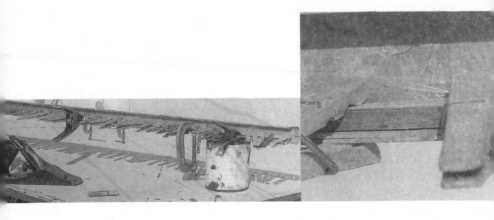

Lamination in progress with a light channel and plenty of white glue and plenty of clamps.

REPAIRING KITE STICKS

One of the advantages of kite sticks with rectangular sections over dowels is apparent when breakage occurs. Breaking a dowel means a new stick, but sticks of rectangular section can be splinted in the field with a minimum of tools, materials, and bother.

MATERIALS
Short sticks of various sections
Thread, white glue

TOOLS
Paper stapler, knife, needle.

Small rasp, file, or piece of coarse sandpaper.

Longerons on sandwich sleds are light in weight and subject to breakage. However, they can be repaired and flight ready in minutes.

Remove any staples, tape, and tie strings for a couple of inches each side of the break. Trim two sticks with the same section as the longerons to 4 inch lengths, spread glue on these splints, and staple them over the fracture. Tie on each side of the break and fly away.

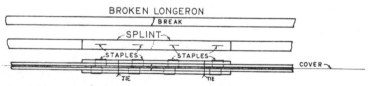

The splint on a delta wing spar should be set on the inner edge of the spar so the trailing edge is not deformed. If the break is at or above the spreader eyelet, turn the stick around and insert it into the slot in the other direction so the splint is near the bottom of the spar.

MODUS OPERANDI

A keel stick or longeron on a Conyne type kite or a box kite may be splinted in the same manner as a wing spar, but since they endure stresses of some magnitude, box spars are called for. Placing the splints on the correct side of the spar and sanding or filing when needed will accomplish a repair that does not disturb the configuration of the kite.

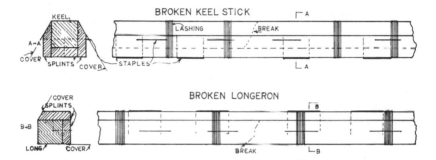

If the break occurs in an area where the spar is partially surrounded by the kite covering, placing the splints as shown will keep the covering from distortion at the repair site. After the splints are glued and stapled on the spar, they should be lashed at a couple of locations each side of the fracture with thread and glue. This will allow the kite to be immediately flown without fear of staples pulling out or wet glue releasing. The repair should be stronger than the rest of the spar.

Kiter's repair kit .

104

MATERIALS

Many materials are specified for construction of kites in this book, so there may be some value in a listing under the various catagories.

Coverings

- Polyethylene plastic bags. Nonporous-drapable-tape or heat seal-needs to be re-enforced with tape-decorate with permanent ink pens-color choice limited-strength fair-readily available-low cost.
- Stressed polyethylene bags. Stronger than trash bags-attractive colors and patterns-available as carryout bags at retail stores.
- Tyvek plastic. Discussed at length in following pages.
- Polyester lining cloth. Strong-medium porosity-wide choice of colors and patterns-medium weight and cost.
- Rip-stop Nylon. Probably the strongest lightest fabric available-expensive.

Framing

- Spruce. Light, strong, straight grain-available at hobby shops in some sizes-expensive.
- Scrap edgings. Available in cabinet shop and lumber outlet scrap bins-must be sawn and shaped by the kiter-many woods suitable inc. pine, fir, and some hard woods-must be light, knot-free, straight grained, etc.
- Dowels. Look for straight grain-roll on level surface for straightness-found

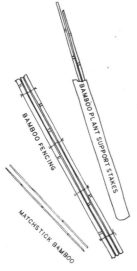

at lumber outlets - OK for cloth with retaining pockets but hard to staple in plastic - cheaper than spruce.

~Bamboo plant support stakes. Excellent for spreaders and braces where taper is OK-strong, light, cheap-find in nursery dept. in lengths 2, 3, & 4 ft.

~Bamboo fencing. For framing where stiffness not required -cheap at bldg. supply store.

~Matchstick bamboo. From old blinds-for use where struct. strength is not required.

~Aluminum tubing. For big kites- buy at bldg. supply-lengths to 12 ft.-dia.$\frac{1}{4}$in. to 1in. -beware of electric wires-fly low.

Tapes

STRAPPING TAPE

~Transparent. For temporary holding-short life in weather.

~Strapping. Strong-weathers poorly.

~Duct tape. Strength fair-stands up to weather and heat well.

DUCT TAPE

Bindings

~Thread. For lashing spars.

~Light twine. For ties and re-enforcements.

~Monofilament line. For "spring" re-strainers.(see page 10)

~Nylon seine twine. For bridles on big kites-glue knots to secure.

105

Metal joiners

~Jumbo paper clips. Make good hooks for spreaders-bend to suit with pliers, two hooks per clip.

~Drapery hooks. A more expensive spreader hook-ready made.

~Brads. Get 17 guage, 1" or $\frac{3}{4}$" long - for joining, especially on box kites.

~Eyelets. For spreader & bridle connections.

~Swivels. For line twist-fast release.

~Bag ties. For fast temporary ties-come with plastic bags-extra ties in produce dept. in super market.

WIRE BRADS

EYELETS

Snap Swivels

BAG TIES

Decorations

~Permanent ink pens. To color plastic bags-get broad tip-refill ink for sale in artist supply.

~Acrylic artist colors. For paper and Tyvek-water mix-waterproof -buy at art supply.

~Vinyl boundary ribbon-1in. wide-vivid colors including florescent-great for tassels and tails-cheap at surveyor's supply.

WIDE TIP MARKING PEN

ACRYLIC ARTIST COLOR

SURVEYOR'S BOUNDARY RIBBON

Adhesives

~White glue. For thread lashing, laminating, repair of wood-glues Tyvek and paper.

~Contact cement. Secures knots-laminating, repairs, etc.

WHITE GLUE

COVERING KITES WITH TYVEK

"Tyvek®is a waterproof paper made of spun-bonded olefin fibers. An excellent material for kitemaking, it can be taped, glued or sewn like cloth...." reads the entry in a kite outlet catalogue. They quote a price that is 25% that of sailcloth nylon while giving a bonus of 19" more width on the Tyvek. They then state that it drapes like cloth and can be decorated with acrylic paint. They also specify type 14, the kind usually used for kites.

This is good news to an old paper-&-paste kite man who is afraid to fly a kite at altitude if it costs more than three dollars. It is also encouraging to those who would rather paint than sew. There is a prevalent bias that a beautiful kite must be sewn, appliqued or quilted a la Betsy Ross. This might be because they last longer in musuems, but the painted beauties from the Orient should attest that there is a place for a brush as well as a needle. And Betsy is the only seamstress in the biographical names section of my dictionary while there are two painters in the Z's alone.

Of course, as in any material, there are problems. It will stretch. Since it seems to be made in layers, it may pull apart at a glued joint. It snags on rough sticks.

Here are ways to use Nylon strapping tape to help remedy some of these problems:

1. Preventing stretch and pull-away in a box kite cell. Tape can be applied as shown, the joint glued, short pieces of tape com-

Cell line

$\frac{3}{4}$"tape   Inside of cell

$1\frac{1}{2}$" glue tab   2" joint tab

pleting the circuits, and the tabs then
folded over the tape and glued. The
joint patches are then applied on the outside
and the cell turned inside out so all is hidden. Or
the joint can be fixed first, then the edge tapes so
one piece makes the circuit and overlaps itself. Then
turn cell inside out after glueing the tabs.

2. Reinforcing stub wings et al..
   Include glue tabs on the outboard edges and tape
   and glue. Tape in the inboard hem of a sandwich
   type wing helps too and also in the wing spar hem
   of a delta wing. Add Tyvek tape patches to joints
   of wings and flares and fins and faces, especially
   at the tops and bottoms. For other hints see the
   Bristol Box, pages 68-9. All the above applies also
   to Housewrap, Tyvek's poor cousin.

For kites that specify plastic bags, increase the dimensions by 25 to 50% or more for Tyvek. It is heavier and stronger.

The final touches of acrylic paint are applied to the sky side of Thunderbird for the benefit of those viewing from very high places.

KITEMAKING TOOLS

Kites can be made with a minimum of tools if necessary. A knife and a pair of scissors are all that are required for a simple kite, but, if more elaborate designs are to be attempted, it is better that the kite builder be adequately equipped.

The handiest tool for a kiter is a power saw to rip his own kite sticks. It drastically reduces one of the highest costs of kite building. The raw materials, straight grained edgings, are free. They can be found in scrap bins at lumber outlets and cabinet shops.

It is possible to cut a kite stick from an edging with no more than a coping saw and vice, if the stick is smoothed afterward with a plane, so three more tools are added to the list.

The next tool is a drill, hand or electric, and a set of drill bits from $\frac{1}{16}$ to $\frac{3}{8}$ inches. These facilitate the using of bamboo plant support stakes for framing and are useful in many other ways in kite building.

Another tool that helps the process along is an eyelet or grommet punch, especially on delta wing kites. It is a one function tool so far as kites are concerned, but, since its cost is low, it is a good investment.

It is better to heat seal bag plastic than to use tape. This requires a burning, soldering, or clothes pressing iron. Keep paper between the iron and the plastic. Use the edge of a pressing iron for a neat seam.

The remainder of the tools are found in most homes. A special implement that should be mentioned is a kite clamp, known in the days of yore as a clothes pin. After their original use is forgotten, kiters will be using them for gluing splints etc. Every kite kit should have some.

MODUS OPERANDI

Below are most of the tools used to build the kites and and other gear in the book. Most of the pictures were clipped from sales flyers left on the doorstep, so, if the kiter does not have them in his kit, he should have little trouble finding them for sale at bargain prices

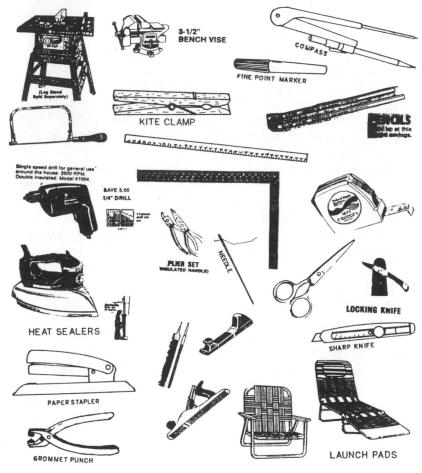

3-1/2"
BENCH VISE

COMPASS

FINE POINT MARKER

(Leg Stand
Sold Separately)

KITE CLAMP

PENCILS

Single speed drill for general use
around the house. 2500 RPM.
Double Insulated. Model #7004.

SAVE 5.00
1/4" DRILL

PLIER SET
(INSULATED HANDLE)

NEEDLE

HEAT SEALERS

LOCKING KNIFE

SHARP KNIFE

PAPER STAPLER

GROMMET PUNCH

LAUNCH PADS

110

KITES AND THE WIND

Kiters, like Mr. Dick, who fly their kites of an evening, have several things in their favor. The low sun may illuminate the face of the kite, so it can be seen, instead of presenting a darkened silhouette to the beholder. The winds have quieted, and, instead of the variable conditions of midday, typically, a steady body of cool dense air seems to flow across the landscape, holding kites in place against the sky:

.... As idle as a painted ship
Upon a painted ocean.   S.T. Coleridge, *Ancient Mariner*

The kiter can tie down and stroll around the neighborhood, seeing his kite from various angles, finding it in the same spot, a wonderful time for contemplation. Do not stroll too far or stay away too long, as breezes of an evening have been known to vanish as mysteriously as they have appeared, leaving the kite on a slack line, desperately seeking a sky hook.

The afternoon winds are fun too. The shifts and lulls keep the kiter from dozing, and, every so often, a thermal of rising air catches the kite and elevates it far overhead, accompanied by soaring birds who well know the value of a free ride.

It is a pity that tradition classes kiting as a springtime activity. The winds of spring are as fickle as a faithless lover, often blowing from too much to too little within a span of minutes, with shifts that generously include all points of the compass. Summer winds are more reliable, usually prevailing in one direction with an abundance of kite and spirit lifting thermals. Autumn can be off again on again with breathless Indian summer, although there are many fine flying days. And in climes with mild winters like California, kiting can be carried on for twelve months of the year with little danger of frostbite. My mind pictures a sleigh or a speeding skier tacking across snow covered fields or frozen lake, towed by a Charvolant arrangement of guided kites. Kiting in the snow? It might be fun.

Charles Dickens's setting of a green hill for Mr. Dick's kite flying presented an idyllic image, but his description ommitted details that would be of interest to the practical kiter; like the size of the hill, the wind direction, and the part of the hill where Mr. Dick and David were located. If the hill were small, a mere hummock on the landscape, it matters little where they sat, but, assuming a more imposing eminence; we can, perhaps, reconstruct the scene from the evidence. The kite was large and was flying high in a light evening breeze, which indicates the presence of a rising air current. The air was quiet or without turbulence. These conditions eliminate the lee and crown of the hill since both locations are subject to down drafts and turbulence. They must have been on the windward side near the bottom of the slope, where Mr. Dick, experienced kiter that he was, relied on an ascending cushion of air to support his Memorial laden kite. The old fellow might have been slightly mad, but he did not suffer from a lack of intelligence. He knew the wind.

An offshore wind is often a disappointment with a long line and not much altitude. An onshore breeze does more for you as air rises over the higher and warmer land. One can observe hang-gliders and radio controlled model sail planes utilizing this phenomenon to keep their crafts aloft for long periods of time. Fly from a beach, below cliffs, in a moderate onshore breeze, and your kite will perform at its best.

Domina Jalbert designed the parafoil to fly in hundred mile per hour winds, but the recreational kiter is better off to stay indoors during winds over force six, and even six can be uncomfortable and too much for most kites. Kites fly best in light to moderate winds. High winds exert excessive drag to the air foil to cause distortion, which sends kites out of control, and drag on the line causes altitude inhibiting sag. A kiter from England wrote about his Pagoda taking top honors in a kite fly held during a gale, the only kite to stay aloft. That Pagoda must have been a well built kite and have had a sturdy spreader.

Low altitude winds cause the most problems for kites. The rough ground air has kites cutting capers at the time and place most likely to cause damage. To minimize these hazards, locate your launch pad away from obstructions-trees, buildings, cliffs, etc.-; upwind to avoid turbulence, downwind to avoid kite traps. Disregarding the rules, the author launched a Sandwich Sled Delta-a kite tolerant toward turbulence –in a narrow canyon from a small parking lot surrounded by tall trees, just to see if it could be done. The wind was from the east in the canyon floor but blew from a westerly direction above the cliffs, with the kite soaring on 2000 feet of line at a near vertical angle. As they say, "When there's a wind, there's a way."

Preoccupation with the marvelous ocean of air that surrounds us will continue so long as humankind persists in utilizing its properties. If we are diligent in our hobbies, vocations, and sciences, we may someday know as much of the motions of this remarkable fluid as the seagulls.

Physical conditioning can be combined with a hobby if the proper equipment is at hand.

Photo by Waine Landers.

113

FLYING WITH FLAIR

We fly kites for personal satisfaction, but there is an inherant exhibitionist character to the activity. After all, the pleasure we derive from our graceful creation is enhanced by others sharing in it . So, to use the parlance of the entertainment business, if we are putting on a show, it is no crime to class up our act a little.

Consider, for instance, the basic procedure of launching. You are on a beach preparing to send your spangled beauty aloft. You can dash off in Hollywood style with line in hand, either stumbling over reclining bodies if you are watching the kite, or dragging the kite through the flotsam and jetsam if you are watching your step. This scenario is understandable, since running to get a kite aloft is standard procedure for the unintiated, regardless of the di - rection of the wind. There is a tale of a television cam - era crew who requested that the kites be flown in the opposite direction because of the sun's glare.

Therefore, let us find ways to accomplish our objec - tive with elegance and aplomb. A steady onshore wind at your back. Toss the kite in the air, and, with a supple wrist and a series of jerks, work the kite skyward. With a little practice, the kite can be made to dance along a few feet above the ground as you let out line, pausing over selected sunbathers as you execute a chasse, and, a moment before crashing the life guard's tower, with a flick of the wrist, send it streaking skyward, afterburners aflame. Even more impressive is to perform these exercises while seated in the sand or on a beach chair.

Retrieving a kite can also be done with style. Take in line slowly as the kite nears to avoid overfly, with only an occasional sidestep to correct a yaw, and bring it deftly to hand before it touches the ground. It also shows good form to accomplish this maneuver while seated. In fact, it can offer a challenging test of skill in turbulent air, but a "super" stable kite like a Stacked Deltas and practice will enable you to make it look easy .

If you have more than one kite along, it makes a pretty picture to fly them at the same altitude a short distance apart. Tie them down and let them fly themselves while you loll in the sand. Or loft a few in tandem, on a strong line, pre-readied and wound on a reel. It is more effec- tive if the kites are not too far apart and are different in design. If accomplished smoothly, there should be some resemblance to clowns emerging from a Volkwagen.

Beware the helpful bystanders! They account for sig- nifigantly more broken kites and tangled string than gale winds and run at least a respectable second to kite eating trees.

The ultimate in kite showmanship is flying guided kites in train, but, from some perspectives, the activity seems a bit athletic. 15 mile per hour winds are required, stray kite lines cause all to go awry, and there is little time for conversation or contemplation. For a more phlegmatic life style, rig a Winged "W" or a Stacked Deltas Sled with 150 feet of double line. Tie the ends of the lines together, put it around your back. These kites will perform in any wind that will keep a kite aloft, and the movements are deliberate and easy to control. They will make all the fig- ures and are particularly effective at hovering at the extremes of the side tacks, where they will hang for long periods of time.

So pick a surf line or a path where people are approach- ing and tease them with a hovering kite or an appended tail. They are almost sure to smile as they pass, and many will stop to ask how it is done, an amusing way to meet new people.

BIBLIOGRAPHY

There are a prolifery of kite books covering the several areas and levels of kiting, but the following list, like this book, is not set up to tell you "all you ev r want to know about kiting". These books give fairly comprehensive overviews of the subject and explanations of some terms, names, and illustrations used so loosely in the text, force 6, Harry Sauls, et al.

Historical references for the days when kites ruled the skies in this country can be found by consulting the *Periodical Index* for the years 1890 to 1910. Fascinating reading. The original issues or microfilm copies can be found in libraries. Current developments can be followed in the bulletins of the American Kiteflyers Association (AKA) and the magazines Kite Lines and American Kites, all of interest to kiters.

Brummitt, Wyatt. *Kites; A Golden Handbook Guide*. 1971. Golden Press. Out of print but in all the libraries and still available by mail order through KITE LINES magazine. A good overview of kiting. Instructions are general and usually correct. A well organized book.

Pelham, David. *The Penguin Book of Kites*. 1976. Penguin Books, Inc. Extensive coverage. General instructions. Continues from where Brummitt left off.

Newman, Lee Scott & Jay Hartley Newman. *Kite Craft: The History and Processes of Kitemaking Through-out the World*. 1976. Crown Publishers, Inc. The title overstates the book. A fair overview, but many pictures of oriental kites do little for a kiter. Directions calling for thirty two $\frac{3}{16}$" square sticks for a 3ft. box kite is a bit on the side of overkill. A sturdy box, but will it fly?

Hart, Clive. *Kites: An Historical Survey.* 1982. Paul P. Appel. Mt. Vernon, NY. Revision of a 1967 title. It tells a a lot of old but not much recent history A new revision is needed.

Rowlands, Jim. *The Big Book of Kites.* An English kiteman comes up with some good construction ploys – the best part of the book. The 30 kite designs may be, as stated, original but not, perchanch, revolutionary. Getting some of the directions to jibe with the drawings is sometimes difficult.

Gregor, Margaret. *Kites for Everyone.* 1984. & *More Kites for Everyone.* 1990. An all around approach which includes kites from simple to advanced, traditional and avant-garde, with good construction tips. Self published too. I wondered about this lady but later discovered the man of the house was also into kites so, I can preserve some semblance of my tattered chauvinism.

OTHER PUBLICATIONS

Kiting: Journal of the (AKA)-American Kitefliers Association, 1559 Rockville Pike, Rockville, MD 20852. Comes out six times a year to members. It keeps kiters abreast of flies, conventions, trends, kite outlets, etc.. Join now. Membership $15 per yr.. $2 extra for each added family member.

BIBLIOGRAPHY

*Kite Lines: Quarterly Journal of the Worldwide Kite-
ing Community.* 8807 Liberty Rd., Randallstown, MD
21133. Current developments in kiting everywhere, from
kite festivals to book and kite reviews plus mail order
books. Some original back issues available or microfilms
of them and all issues of its predecessor, *Kite Tales* – a
treasure house of kite lore.

American Kite: 480 Clementina St, San Francisco, CA
94103. A new entrant to the field with a western slant.
Good things on the orient too plus articles from Ingraham and other kiters. The more the merrier. A quarterly magazine.

POETRY

APOLOGIA
by
Neil Thorburn

What was it that at tender age
Impelled me to pre-empt a page
Of newsprint from an old edition
And beg my parent a petition
To show me how to cross the sticks,　5
To notch the ends, and then to fix
The cover and to tie the strings,
The bridle, tail and fastenings?

Did spirit spurn the clod and stone
And fret its cage of flesh and bone?　10
Or was I seeking adulation
Achieved in sleepy levitation?
Yet, those of Freud might well uncover
A darker drive like hating Mother,
Or was the quest oblivion　15
As Icarus striving toward the sun?

No matter what the cause or call,
I rolled some line into a ball
And lifting up my frail creation
Proceeded with some trepidation　20
To hie to field o'er stem and stubble
And reel some line out on the double,
Then run and pull with main and might;
And lo! It rose in glorious flight.

Nirvana! Yea, the soul doth sing　25
In harmony to humming string,
Responding to the trilling pull
To perne in gyre with snowy gull,
Then scale the heights unto the sun,
Make nature, mind, and body one;　30
And thus, an early aspiration
Begot a permanent fixation.

Far down the shearing streams of time
In temperate, chill, or tropic clime,
The humor holds, and should I mark　35
A beach or hill, a field or park,
I slow to scan the flags and trees
To fix the force and course of breeze,
And, should conditions feel but fair
You'll spy a flying object there.　40

Should my pursuit provoke a twit
From some untutored vocal wit,
I'll claim my kick shows no more kinks
Than chipping balls across a links;
Nor does it any way besmear　45
Our much abused terrestrial sphere;
Pollute the air, infest the sea,
Or broadcast harsh cacophony.

More oft' a little child will linger
Pointing with a pudgy finger.   50
A curious lad may ask me why
It hangs so still or soars so high.
A lissome lass may stay her stride
To stand a moment by my side.
One cannot build nor buy nor lease   55
So sure a conversation piece.

A man kneels near a coral reef.
He frames a pliant breadfruit leaf
With fronds of palm so deftly put.
His twine he twists from coconut.   60
An angling gear is his design
Which could lead pundits to opine,
"The primal moves in aviation
Were made as aids to occupation."

Top hallowed hill in old Cathay   65
A holy man observes the sway
Of silken foil. He notes the tail.
It bodes if crops will grow or fail.
The hummer speaks for sires of yore.
They prophesy of peace or war;   70
And so, flight annals from the east
Report the presence of the priest.

"But Han Hsin's hummers", sayeth the seer,
"Were flown to foster doubt and fear".
Conyne's and Hargrave's new designs   75
Intrigued the military minds.
The Wrights' invention, in its turn,
Is made to maim and kill and burn.
Another beauty swells the van
Of inhumanities to man.   80

A beauty soiled is beauty still,
So leave me on an open hill,
Where I can ply my archaism
And practice gentle pantheism;
There, to see my craft ephemeral   85
Aspiring on a lofting thermal;
Then, with fair and faithful Caurus,
I join the brotherhood in chorus.

Hail Hinze and Mel and Val and Grauel!
Praise Hargrave, Eddy, Baden-Powell,   90
Conyne, Scott, and let us hallow
Franklin, Jalbert, and Rogallo,
Brummitt, Ingraham, Bell and Jue,
Baldwin, Wrights and Bigge too,
Moulton, Pelham, Brown and Lee!   95
God bless our snug fraternity!

NOTES
(For those unaquainted with kite lore)

8. My first kite. A burn door 3 sticker.
12. I seem to have an admiring audience when I "fly".
16. The generation gap.
26. Gary Hinze estimates wind speed from the pitch of the hum. He calibrated it with his wind guage and violin.
28. Yeats, the Irish poet, had birds and souls perning in gyre — flying in a spiral. The white bird sybolizes the soul.
32. Contagious but usually benign.
33. The jet streams — defined as shear winds.
38. The Beauforte Wind Scale that makes use of flags, trees, etc. in estimating wind velocity.
40. Kites are sometimes identified as U F O's. If the observer can't tell a kite from a jaybird, the definition applies.
41. e.g. Did your wife tell you to go fly a kite?

56. Elderly gentlemen and little old ladies too.
61. Wayne Baldwin descibed such a kite in KITE TALES; Fall,1977.
69. Most honorable ancestors.
74. General Hsin, according to legend, "spooked" an enemy army by lofting hummer kites at night.
76. I first knew the Conyne as the French War Kite.
84. See line 30.
87 "Caurus", Latin for NW. wind. It prevails in the Santa Clara Valley.
88. "Brotherhood", kiters— present, past, affiliated, free lance, or anyone else who loves kites.
95. Kiters-contemporary and of yore. This is not intended as a Hall of Fame. The names were chosen for rhyme, meter, alliteration, and assonance.

SYMBIOSIS
by
H.B. Alexander

Oh, I have lofted you my friend,
Upon the summer's gentle wind
And fought your frantic pitches, yaws,
In bleak December's icy claws
And I have flown you tailess, free
Above the sparkling springtime sea,
And decked your wings with streamers gold
In blue October's stinging cold;
In every weather we are found-
You in the sky, I on the ground.

Through our umbilical of thread
My hand and ears have often read
The joyous humming, thrumming lays
Of poets from long bygone days;
I've given you my woe and care
To have it scattered on the air;
And though I know that we are bound-
You to my hand, I to the ground-
Still we both know that we are free
Bound to each other, you and me.

Shakespear's Sonnet #18 - original version.
Discovered by H.B. Alexander

Shall I fly thee upon a summer's day
Thou art so lovely and so temperate
Rough winds do shake the darling buds of May,
And summer's lease hath all too short a date.
Sometimes too hot the eye of heaven shines   5
And often is his gold complexion dimmed,
And every kite from high sometimes declines,
By chance or nature's changing course untrimmed;
But thy eternal climbing shall not fade
Nor lose possession of that height thou gainest, 10
Nor shall birds brag thou soarest in their shade
When on the braided flying line thou straineth;
   So long as I can breathe or my eyes see
   I'll feed thee line, for this gives height to thee.

3. Shakespeare knew rough winds usually come in March but was desperate for a rhyme.
5. More evidence of the bird's aversion to strong sunlight. Cf.(Hamlet, I, ii ,67.) The paper of that day probably lost strength in the hot sun.
6. "Dimmed" or reduced by thunderheads. As Shakespeare had never heard of Ben Franklin and was no fool, he would not fly a kite near thunderheads.
7. Reference here is to the phenomenon of wind velocity diminishing before a change in direction. Alternatively, considered in context with the preceeding line, Shakespeare may have been referring to downdrafts. Either phenomenon causes kites to "decline" or lose altitude.
11. "Birds" in the original draft read kites a type of bird for which man-made kites are named in English; this might have been interpreted as another's kite topping Shakespeare's God forbid. Shakespeare too, so he changed it.
13. Cf. note ln.5 supra

Poems by
Bernice B. Turner

My Kite Goes Free

My kite is free
  it's flying alone;
It won't be returning
  to my home.

The wind has taken
  it far away,
And it's going to enjoy
  long hours of play.

My Kite

I tossed my kite
  into the sky;
It fluttered happily
  and seemed to sigh.

I tugged it gently-
  let out some string,
and moments later,
  it began to sing.

The Ballet in the Sky 1

The grace of the ballet
  in the sky
Is most delightful
  to mind and eye.
The lyrical swoops
  In tune with the wind
Gives a feeling of charm
  as they all begin.

Exhilarating dips and dives
  make the kites come alive
The kiter deftly maneuvers
  two lines
As music directs his
  rhythm and time

1. Dedicated to Olan and his Rainbow Kites.

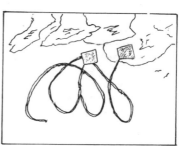

Over and over
  I've heard folks say,
"I've never seen kites
  behave that way!"
They watch in wonder,
  thrilled with the sight.
It's harmony orchestrated;
  it's beauty in flight.

INDEX

Underlined page numbers indicate photographs.

INDEX

Outlanders, visitors or immigrants, often stroll in our parks. They may stop and chat with a kiteflyer if he has a distinctive kite. (See page 120, lines 55-6). A little urging will elicit the word for kite in their native languages. The following is a list of words the author has remembered or looked up. A few secondary definitions are included: English. kite. Small hawk. Sharper. Rubber check.. Sail. Any additions or corrections will be appreciated.

German: Papier-Drache(n)
Dutch: Vlieger (flyer), Draak
Norwegian: Glente; Drake (dragon)
Danish: Glente; Drage
Finnish; Leija
Polish: Latawiek
Russian: ЗМей - změy??
Hungarian: Papir Sarkany (dragon)
Turkish: Ucurmaktma
Chinese: Fēngjěne or Fùngjàng (flier)
Tagalog: Bulador; Sapi sapi
Estonian: Tuulelome (dragon)
Arab: Taya, Tayyara (plane); Waraq
Indian: Patung
Malay; Layna
Japanese: Tako; Kanbori; Shiyen
Ethiopia: Mashawcha

French: Cerf Volant (click beetle)
Italian: Aquilone (large eagle)
Spanish: Cometa; Papalote (Mex.);
    Barrelete (C.A.)
Portuguese; Papagalo de papel (paper
    yellow parrot)
Slovac; Sarkan (dragon)
Rumanian: Zmeu; Draya
Armenian: Tsin
Lao: Wow
Indonesian: Layang layang
Korean: Yon
Viet: Cal dieù
Nepali: Chīl; Sikaripanki; Urāunne
    changa (boy's kite); Guddi
Esperanto: Kajto
Persian: Badbadak

Printed in Hong Kong